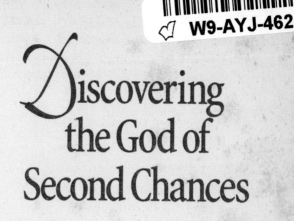

Discovering the God of Second Chances

KAY ARTHUR
PETE De LACY

HARVEST HOUSE PUBLISHERS

EUGENE, OREGON

Cover by Koechel Peterson & Associates, Inc., Minneapolis, Minnesota

The New Inductive Study Series
DISCOVERING THE GOD OF SECOND CHANCES
Copyright © 2005 by Precept Ministries International
Published by Harvest House Publishers
Eugene, Oregon 97402
www.harvesthousepublishers.com

Library of Congress Cataloging-in-Publication Data
  Arthur, Kay, 1933–
  Discovering the God of second chances / Kay Arthur and Pete De Lacy.
      p. cm. — (The new inductive study series)
  ISBN 978-0-7369-0359-2 (pbk.)
  ISBN 978-0-7369-3570-8 (eBook)
  1. Bible. O.T. Obadiah—Textbooks. 2. Bible. O.T. Joel—Textbooks. 3. Bible. O.T. Amos—Textbooks. 4. Bible. O.T. Jonah—Textbooks. I. De Lacy, Pete. II. Title. III. Series.
  BS1595.55.A87 2005
  224'.9'0071—dc22   2005001502

Printed in the United States of America

14   15   16   17   18   19   / BP-CF /   12   11   10   9   8   7   6

CONTENTS

∾∾∾∾

How to Get Started...

Reading directions is sometimes difficult and hardly ever enjoyable! Most often you just want to get started. Only if all else fails will you read the instructions. We understand, but please don't approach this study that way. These brief instructions are a vital part of getting started on the right foot! These few pages will help you immensely.

FIRST

As you study Obadiah, Joel, Amos, and Jonah, you will need four things in addition to this book:

1. A Bible that you are willing to mark in. The marking is essential. An ideal Bible for this purpose is *The New Inductive Study Bible (NISB)*. The *NISB* is in a single-column text format with large, easy-to-read type, which is ideal for marking. The margins of the text are wide and blank for note taking.

The *NISB* also has instructions for studying each book of the Bible, but it does not contain any commentary on the text, nor is it compiled from any theological stance. Its purpose is to teach you how to discern truth for yourself through the inductive method of study. (The various charts and maps that you will find in this study guide are taken from the *NISB*.)

Whichever Bible you use, just know you will need to mark in it, which brings us to the second item you will need...

2. A fine-point, four-color ballpoint pen or various colored fine-point pens that you can use to write in your Bible. Office supply stores should have these.

3. Colored pencils or an eight-color leaded Pentel pencil.

4. A composition book or a notebook for working on your assignments or recording your insights.

SECOND

1. As you study these four minor prophets, you will be given specific instructions for each day's study. These should take you between 20 and 30 minutes a day, but if you spend more time than this, you will increase your intimacy with the Word of God and the God of the Word.

If you are doing this study in a class and you find the lessons too heavy, simply do what you can. To do a little is better than to do nothing. Don't be an all-or-nothing person when it comes to Bible study.

Remember, anytime you get into the Word of God, you enter into more intensive warfare with the devil (our enemy). Why? Every piece of the Christian's armor is related to the Word of God. And our one and only offensive weapon is the sword of the Spirit, which is the Word of God. The enemy wants you to have a dull sword. Don't cooperate! You don't have to!

2. As you read each chapter, train yourself to ask the "5 W's and an H": who, what, when, where, why, and how. Asking questions like these helps you see exactly what the Word of God is saying. When you interrogate the text with the 5 W's and an H, you ask questions like these:

a. **What** is the chapter about?

b. **Who** are the main characters?

c. **When** does this event or teaching take place?

d. **Where** does this happen?

e. **Why** is this being done or said?

f. **How** did it happen?

3. The "when" of events or teachings is very important and should be marked in an easily recognizable way in your Bible. You could mark it with a clock (like the one shown here) 🕐 in the margin of your Bible beside the verse where the time phrase occurs. You may want to underline or color the references to time in one specific color.

4. You will be given certain key words to mark throughout these four Old Testament books. This is the purpose of the colored pencils and the colored pens. If you will develop the habit of marking your Bible in this way, you will find it will make a significant difference in the effectiveness of your study and in how much you remember.

A **key word** is an important word that the author uses repeatedly in order to convey his message to his reader. Certain key words will show up throughout each book; others will be concentrated in specific chapters or segments of a book. When you mark a key word, you should also mark its synonyms (words that mean the same thing in the context) and any pronouns *(he, his, she, her, it, we, they, us, our, you, their, them)* in the same way you have marked the key word. We will give you suggestions for ways to mark key words in your daily assignments.

You can use colors or symbols or a combination of colors and symbols to mark words for easy identification. However, colors are easier to distinguish than symbols. When we use symbols, we keep them very simple. For example, you could color *repent* yellow but put a red diagram like this over it repent because it indicates a change of mind.

When marking key words, mark them in a way that is

easy for you to remember.

If you devise a color-coding system for marking key words throughout your Bible, then when you look at the pages of your Bible, you will see instantly where a key word is used.

You might want to make yourself a bookmark listing the words you want to mark along with their colors and/or symbols.

5. AT A GLANCE charts are located at the end of each book's study. As you complete your study of each chapter, record the main theme of that chapter under the appropriate chapter number. The main theme of a chapter is what the chapter deals with the most. It may be an event or a particular subject or teaching.

If you will fill out the AT A GLANCE charts as you progress through the study, you will have a complete synopsis of the books when you are finished. If you have a *New Inductive Study Bible*, you will find the same charts in your Bible (pages 1461, 1478, 1482, and 1487). If you record your chapter themes there, you'll have them for a ready reference.

6. Always begin your study with prayer. As you do your part to handle the Word of God accurately, you must remember that the Bible is a divinely inspired book. The words that you are reading are truth, given to you by God so you can know Him and His ways more intimately. These truths are divinely revealed.

> For to us God revealed them through the Spirit; for the Spirit searches all things, even the depths of God. For who among men knows the thoughts of a man except the spirit of the man which is in him? Even so the thoughts of God no one knows except the Spirit of God (1 Corinthians 2:10-11).

Therefore ask God to reveal His truth to you as He leads

and guides you into all truth. He will if you will ask.

7. Each day when you finish your lesson, meditate on what you saw. Ask your heavenly Father how you should live in light of the truths you have just studied. At times, depending on how God has spoken to you through His Word, you might even want to record these "Lessons for Life" in the margin of your Bible next to the text you have studied. Simply put "LFL" in the margin of your Bible and then, as briefly as possible, record the lesson for life that you want to remember.

THIRD

This study is set up so that you have an assignment for every day of the week—so that you are in the Word daily. If you work through your study in this way, you will find it more profitable than doing a week's study in one sitting. Pacing yourself this way allows time for thinking through what you learn on a daily basis!

The seventh day of each week differs from the other six days. The seventh day is designed to aid group discussion; however, it's also profitable if you are studying this book individually.

The "seventh" day is whatever day in the week you choose to finish your week's study. On this day, you will find a verse or two for you to memorize and STORE IN YOUR HEART. Then there is a passage to READ AND DISCUSS. This will help you focus on a major truth or major truths covered in your study that week.

To assist those using the material in a Sunday school class or a group Bible study, there are QUESTIONS FOR DISCUSSION OR INDIVIDUAL STUDY. Even if you are not doing this study with anyone else, answering these questions would be good for you.

If you are in a group, be sure every member of the class, including the teacher, supports his or her answers and insights from the Bible text itself. Then you will be handling the Word of God accurately. As you learn to see what the text says and compare Scripture with Scripture, the Bible explains itself.

Always examine your insights by carefully observing the text to see what it *says*. Then, before you decide what the passage of Scripture *means,* make sure that you interpret it in the light of its context. Scripture will never contradict Scripture. If it ever seems to contradict the rest of the Word of God, you can be certain that something is being taken out of context. If you come to a passage that is difficult to understand, reserve your interpretations for a time when you can study the passage in greater depth.

The purpose of the THOUGHT FOR THE WEEK is to share with you what we consider to be an important element in your week of study. We have included it for your evaluation and, hopefully, for your edification. This section will help you see how to walk in light of what you learned.

Books in The New Inductive Study Series are survey courses. If you want to do a more in-depth study of a particular book of the Bible, we suggest you do a Precept Upon Precept Bible study course on that book. You may obtain more information on these courses by contacting Precept Ministries International at 800-763-8280, visiting our website at www.precept.org, or filling out and mailing the response card in the back of this book.

DISCOVERING THE GOD OF SECOND CHANCES

What do you do when you've blown it? Can you recover? Can God still use you, or will He consign you to the dustbin of life?

Seven hundred years had passed since Israel covenanted with God to obey Him. Israel had blown it. They had committed adultery, worshipping idols and forsaking the God who had brought them out of slavery in Egypt and into the land of promise.

What would God do with Israel? Would they get a second chance?

God sent prophets with a message of judgment for sin and a call to repent, to turn from their ways—a message that also held hope for the future. The four prophets you will study in this booklet all help us learn about the second chances that God gave Israel and other nations. As we look at the messages of Obadiah, Joel, Amos, and Jonah, remember that they were God's messengers, bringing His Word to turn people toward Him and away from their idols, away from their self-centeredness, away from all that kept them from seeing Him and knowing Him.

Their messages have much in common with today's world. Christians today need to hear this call from God. Some need to return to Him. God also calls to nations today.

He calls us to shape our thinking and behavior by His holy Word delivered through His messengers, the prophets. He calls us to return if we have strayed, to turn to Him in obedience and true worship, for He gives us another chance.

Study with expectancy, Beloved, for God will show you truth through His Holy Spirit that you cannot see in any other way. Look for His personal message to you and your situation, and let it change your life and the lives of those around you. Discover the God of second chances!

A Brief Background for Studying the Prophets

∾∾∾∾∾

In the Bible, we find two kinds of prophets: those whose spoken messages became parts of books of the Bible (mixed in with history) and those whose messages became whole books of the Bible. The Old Testament of the Christian Bible includes four "major prophets" and twelve "minor prophets." Major and minor refer to the length and significance of the books.

The minor prophets can be divided into two groups, preexilic and postexilic, based on whether their messages pertained to times before or after the exile of the southern kingdom of Judah to Babylon from 605 to 536 BC. Obadiah, Joel, Amos, and Jonah are four of the nine preexilic minor prophets. The postexilic prophets, Haggai, Zechariah, and Malachi, are covered in *Opening the Windows of Blessing,* and the rest of the preexilic prophets are the subjects of other booklets of the New Inductive Study Series.

To understand the four prophets in this booklet, let's summarize the historical setting of Israel, God's chosen people, when these four men of God delivered their messages. When Solomon grew old, his many foreign wives turned his heart away from worshipping God alone, and he worshipped foreign gods, sacrificing to idols made with men's hands. This legacy of idolatry plagued Israel from that day forward. After Solomon's death, the nation split into a northern kingdom, usually called Israel, and a southern kingdom, Judah.

The king of the northern kingdom immediately instituted worship of golden calves and other gods, turning away from God's appointed worship system at the temple in Jerusalem. The southern kingdom still had Jerusalem and the temple, but high places and pagan altars dotted the land, pulling the people's hearts toward idol worship.

Into this environment, God sent His prophets to both kings and peoples—the northern kingdom of Israel, the southern kingdom of Judah, and surrounding nations like Assyria. These prophets preached messages that were unique to their circumstances but have common threads. You will discover the themes they share as you study. The four prophets in this study are related by time and circumstance as well as by certain direct statements from God, yet each has a unique message from God for a particular audience at a particular time and for a particular purpose.

In the same way that God had a message in the days of the prophets for the kings and nations to understand, He has a message for you to understand today. Examine your circumstances, your life, and your relationship to God. See how His message through the prophets pierces your heart into your daily living to instruct you, to shape your thinking, to impel you toward a life of worshipping Him. If you have strayed from loving God, from obeying Him, from worshipping Him in spirit and truth, our prayer is that God's message will call you to return to Him and experience a closer walk with the God of second chances.

Seek diligently, Beloved, to understand God's message to you. Meditate on the truths in His holy Word. Bow before your Father in humble adoration at His graciousness toward those who love Him, obey Him, and serve Him.

OBADIAH

INTRODUCTION TO OBADIAH

Obadiah, whose name means "my servant," was a prophet to Judah, the southern kingdom. The date of his writing is obscure and much debated. Some think it was as early as the ninth century BC, during the reign of Jehoram, while others give it a date soon after 586 BC, when the Babylonians took the last of the captives from Judah. But Obadiah brings a message applicable to nations at any time and people of all times. The Scriptures clearly describe Israel's relationship with God and with the surrounding nations.

The title of this booklet is *Discovering the God of Second Chances.* As you study Obadiah, your goal will be to see how God gives second chances. You need to understand how Judah will receive this message. What will the message bring to their spirits? What would it mean to their hopes and dreams?

Look for the principles Obadiah presents about God's dealings with us; they can fill you with hope. Ask how you might use the message of Obadiah to help someone else know that God gives second chances.

Our days so desperately need revival. Our communities need revival. We need a clear, uncompromising message from God of the sureness of right and wrong, of justice, of God's triumph over those who oppress His people.

What will you learn from Obadiah? Will you find hope? Will you find encouragement? Will you find something that will give you solid ground on which to declare, "Thus says the Lord"?

WHAT SHOULD GOD DO WITH THOSE WHO SIN?

God uses different ways to get our attention when we sin. Sometimes God sends another person to us in love to help us see our error and correct our ways. Sometimes He uses less comfortable circumstances to expose our sin in embarrassing ways. Sometimes He delivers a rebuke through His Word as we read God's message and the Holy Spirit quickens our spirit, reproving and correcting us.

Often God used Israel's enemies to show the nation and its kings their sin. But according to the prophet Zechariah, whoever came against Israel, whoever touched Israel, touched the apple of God's eye. Thus God judged nations who afflicted Israel. God might temporarily afflict Israel by another nation, but He also protected Israel in the long term by judging that nation, stopping it in its tracks.

God delivered a message through Obadiah. Will we listen to that message and let it ring in our ears and pierce our hearts? Will we see the love God has for Israel and the justice He imposes on those who harm the one He loves?

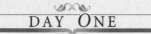

DAY ONE

Obadiah is a short book—just 21 verses. Although prophecy can be complicated, this message isn't; the subject is clear. Quickly read through the book to get the flavor of the message. Then go back and read verse 1 and note who has the vision, what the vision is about, and whom Obadiah is addressing.

Before we do any more in Obadiah, you should understand who Edom is and what its relationship to Israel is. Read the following passages and in a separate notebook, summarize what you learn about Edom: Genesis 25:20-34; 27:1–28:9; Numbers 20:14-21; Deuteronomy 2:1-8,12; 1 Kings 11:14-17; 22:45-47; 2 Kings 8:16-22; Romans 9:10-13; Hebrews 12:15-17.

DAY TWO

Today, read through Obadiah again, marking every reference to *Edom* or *Esau*. As you read and mark key words and phrases in the Word of God, keep focused by asking questions and letting the text give you the answers. Be an investigator—ask Who? What? When? Where? Why? and How? We call these the 5 W's and an H questions. They help you find truth that is there. Marking key words will help you see God's emphasis on people, places, and ideas. Use a symbol or color to distinctively mark each key word. Genesis 25:25 and 30 give a pretty good idea of what color to mark *Esau* and *Edom*.

In your notebook, list what you learn in Obadiah about Edom. Listing what you observe is a good technique to summarize and crystallize what you learn. Writing also helps seal truths in your memory. How does this description of Edom compare to what you saw in the cross references yesterday?

Verse 7 speaks of allies and those at peace. Read the following and note which nations have been allies or at peace with Edom at various times: 1 Samuel 14:47; 2 Samuel 8:11-14; 2 Kings 3:5-27; 1 Chronicles 18:9-13.

DAY THREE

You'll find several key words and phrases that show you clearly what the message of Obadiah is about, so mark them to help you see the message. To help you remember what to mark and how, make a bookmark from an index card. Write the words and mark them on the card. This will also help you keep track when you mark the same words or phrases elsewhere in the Bible. As you observe and mark, remember to ask the 5 W's and an H questions.

Read Obadiah again, and mark any references to God speaking such as *Thus says the* LORD, or *declares the* LORD, references to *Jacob,* and references to *the nations.*[1] Choose a different color or marking symbol for each. Jacob is Israel, so mark both blue, the color of the star of David in Israel's flag. Be sure to mark synonymous references to Jacob besides Israel. One way to mark *the nations* is to color it green and underline in brown. *The nations* refers to Gentiles—any nation other than Israel.

DAY FOUR

Today read through Obadiah and mark *that day* and *the day of the LORD*, which are key in much of prophecy. If you don't know how to color it, color it pink with an orange box. Make sure you include any pronouns or synonyms used for the day of the Lord.

This phrase answers a "when" kind of question, but not by setting a specific date. The time phrase *the day* is quite different from *that day*. *That day* speaks of a future event, while *the day of his/their destruction, distress,* or *disaster* in verses 11-14 speaks of a past event. Mark the phrase *the day of* in these verses differently from the way you mark *that day*. This will help you understand the context of Obadiah's message. What does the Lord say He will do to Edom? What or whom will God use against Edom? When will this happen?

Among the things God declares He will destroy are the "wise men" and "understanding." Read 1 Corinthians 1:18-25. How would you compare these verses to Obadiah 8-9?

DAY FIVE

Read through Obadiah one more time, and this time mark any reference to *Mount Zion* or *My holy mountain.*[2]

Now that you've read Obadiah and marked key words and phrases, let's see what truths we can glean from all your hard work. Make a list of the offenses of Esau/Edom. The wording might sound like it points to the future, but God is reviewing what Edom has already done. What did God tell Edom not to do?

Also read Jeremiah 49:7-22 and record your insights. This cross-reference will show you that God didn't bring a message about Edom through only one prophet. What similar phrases do you see? Note the verb tenses of Jeremiah 49:10,15.

What did God promise Mount Zion in contrast to the mountain of Esau? To whom does Mount Zion refer?

DAY SIX

Read Obadiah 10-14 again. Be sure you have noted and perhaps underlined each *do not* phrase and each *in the day of* phrase. Verse 11 says that "strangers" carried off Jacob's wealth and that Edom stood aloof as "foreigners" entered Jerusalem's gates. The text does not clearly state when this took place, and commentators are divided. However, despite the uncertainty we have about the dating of the events in Obadiah 10-14, is there any uncertainty in verse 10?

What does this say about the certainty of verse 8, even if we don't know that date either? In other words, what understanding, what principle, can we learn from the phrase *declares the* LORD?

When we read, study, and meditate on God's Word, how should we take it—as stories, suggestions, ethical principles rooted in fables? What do you say?

What does God promise Israel?

In light of all you have studied in this short prophecy, what do you think is the central theme (message)? Record it on OBADIAH AT A GLANCE on page 25.

You'll also see on OBADIAH AT A GLANCE a place to record the themes of the three paragraphs of Obadiah.

Determining the main idea in each paragraph and recording it on the AT A GLANCE chart will help you remember the message later when you come back to Obadiah.

The additional chart THE DAY OF THE LORD on pages 26–27 is taken from the *New Inductive Study Bible*. If you record what you learn about the Day of the Lord from Obadiah there and add to it as you study Joel and Amos, you'll have the start of a great topical study of that important prophetic day.

DAY SEVEN

 Store in your heart: Obadiah 21
Read and discuss: Obadiah 1-21; Matthew 25:31-33

QUESTIONS FOR DISCUSSION OR INDIVIDUAL STUDY

- What did Edom do that displeased God?

- What did God say He would do to Edom?

- What will happen in the day of the Lord?

- In what way can we apply this lesson about Edom to our own dealings with Israel?

- How do you think God will deal with nations that behave in the way Edom did? With individuals? How certain is God's justice?

- What kind of relationship to Israel pleases God? How do you view Israel?

∾ How do the warnings God gives to Edom apply to us today? What is God saying about behavior toward His people? What is God saying to you and how you act toward His people?

∾ What do you think the Lord's *attitude* is toward arrogance directed to Him and His Word? What is His *response?*

Thought for the Week

Esau was Jacob's twin brother. While they were still in the womb, God declared that the elder would serve the younger, and what God said came to pass as it always does. Consequently, although Esau was Isaac's firstborn, Esau despised his birthright and sold it to Jacob for a single meal. Later, Jacob deceived Isaac and secured for himself the blessing intended for Esau. While many get stuck on Jacob's methods, the important point is that God said the older would serve the younger, and that's exactly what happened.

If this order was God's decree, Esau should not have been jealous, envious, angry, or malicious toward Jacob. Nor should he have had these attitudes toward God. Esau (Edom) should not have gloated over Jacob's (Israel's) misfortune or in any way participated in the evil that others directed toward Jacob. Jacob, whose name God later changed to Israel, was God's chosen heir to His original promise to Abraham and Isaac. Nothing Esau thought, felt, said, or did would change the truth that God chose Jacob over Esau, because God Himself, not man, chose Jacob. Isaac didn't, Rebekah didn't, and Jacob didn't. God did.

But Esau (Edom) did not accept that truth. The nation of Edom stood by while others plundered Jacob, and then Edom gloated over Jacob's losses and looted and enslaved its remnant (survivors). For this, God would judge Edom. No amount of confidence in their safety, no amount of arrogance would prevent the judgment of God. Judgment for Esau and vindication for Jacob were equally certain.

If a man acts like Esau, seeking revenge for a perceived offense, can he be sure he's right? Can he be sure what has occurred is not part of God's plan to refine us, to shape us, to mold us into the image of Christ?

Think about the injustice of Jesus' death on the cross. He committed no crime and never sinned. But it was according to God's plan. Should Jesus have reviled Jewish or Roman authorities?

In the end, God will judge those who act as Esau did against Israel (as we saw in Obadiah). They act against God, and God will cause the end to be just.

So it is with you and me and everyone else. Justice from God will be the result. Anyone who acts *against* the Word of God will be judged *by* the Word of God (John 12:48). Do not be deceived; God is not mocked. God will be perfectly just. Each of us is accountable before God, and each nation is accountable before God. The day of the Lord is a day of judgment, a day of reckoning, a day of recompense, a day of justice. The wicked will be laid low, and the righteous will be exalted.

God will judge the "brother" of Israel for participating in destroying Israel. The "brother" of Israel who gloats over Israel's misfortunes, who arrogantly stands aloof in their day of trouble and does not lend a hand, will be consumed.

Obadiah's message presents three points to consider, three questions for you to answer for yourself: How do I respond when things don't go the way I think they should? How do I respond to events in Israel's life? And how does God deal with sin?

Your answer to the first question may well determine your answer to the second. Your answer to the third should guide your answers to the first two. "For thus says the LORD of hosts, 'After glory He has sent me against the nations which plunder you, for he who touches you, touches the apple of His eye'" (Zechariah 2:8).

OBADIAH AT A GLANCE

Theme of Obadiah: Judgment is comming for Edom God will judge Esau

SEGMENT DIVISIONS

		PARAGRAPH THEMES	
		VERSES 1-9 Obadiah's Vision the God Concerning Edom How God will distroy Edom God is angry because of what happened in Isiria! the violence	**Author:** Obadiah **Date:** Day of the Lord **Purpose:** Reminder of what is to come
		VERSES 10-14 That you stood aloof that strangers carried off his welth the day of disaster you will be covered with shame And you will be cut off forever Do not rejoice over the sons of Judah. the nation of Iseria!	**Key Words:** the day day of the Lord Edom (Esau) Jacob (Judah) the nations Mount Zion (My holy mountain) declares the Lord (or any phrase having to do with the Lord speaking or reporting)
		VERSES 15-21 Because, just as you Drank of my Holy Mountain, as you have done it will be done unto you. Your dealings will return on your own head. All nations will drink continually the house of Esau will be a stubble	

they will Set them of fire and Comsume them

the Kindom will be the Lord's

REFERENCE	HOW IT IS DESCRIBED

WHAT HAPPENS IN NATURE	SIGNS OF BEGINNING OR END

JOEL

INTRODUCTION TO JOEL

When calamity comes, it can bring anguish, pain, and destruction. But is that all, or does it also bring something else, something positive? Joel has the answer—a word from the Lord. How does the Lord want us to respond to calamity?

Joel, like Obadiah, was a prophet to Judah, the southern kingdom of the Hebrew nation. And like Obadiah, Joel doesn't say when he wrote. Opinions vary about the date of his message, and the estimates range over many centuries. However, we need to focus on the message—the timeless truths of God's Word we can apply to our lives—not speculation about things God sovereignly has chosen not to reveal.

Joel, like most prophets, preached a message designed to expose sin and turn hearers back to the Lord. His message referred to judgment of sin (calamity), but he always intended to turn people back from sin, to encourage them to return to the Lord, to show them that God was giving them a second chance.

Peter quoted Joel in Acts in the midst of one of the great revivals of all history. How will Joel strike your heart? What will God say to you from the message of Joel, whose name means "Jehovah is God"?

Tell Your Sons About It

When something extraordinary happens, we tell stories about it. It becomes the topic of ongoing conversation and sometimes works its way into folklore and history. Succeeding generations hear these stories and learn from them. This is what God is telling Israel through Judah. Don't let this story die…every generation must know…you must tell your children and grandchildren.

DAY ONE

We'll spread our study of Joel over three weeks, covering one chapter a week. Because we build interpretation (our understanding of Scripture) on sound observation, we'll begin observing Joel 1 today.

Read through Joel 1 today, and as you read, mark the following key words or phrases: *locust,*[1] *day of the* LORD, *sackcloth, the house of the* LORD *(of your God)*, and *the land.*[2] Be sure to make a bookmark of key words and phrases, marking the words there as you will in the text. As you turn pages or move to another chapter or book, you can refer to this bookmark and remain consistent.

Think about what you are observing as you read and mark these key words and phrases, and ask Who? What? When? Where? Why? and How? The text has the answers, and you'll find yourself digging in to discover what the chapter is all about, not just marking words.

DAY TWO

Now what in the world is going on? According to Joel 1:2,4, what has happened in the land? What land is Joel referring to? Does the text give you any clues? *Israel*

How are the people of God supposed to prepare for the oncoming calamity? On separate paper or in your notebook, make a chart with the following headings, list the various groups of people this chapter mentions, and explain what God tells each of them to do and why.

THE PEOPLE   WHAT THEY ARE TO DO   WHY THEY ARE TO DO IT

DAY THREE

If you didn't mark references to *the house of the LORD*, go back and do so. If you learn significant things from marking these references, record them in your notebook.

Now move through the chapter and mark its topical divisions. In other words, note when God addresses various groups of people and when the subject changes—when He moves from one thing to another. Then in the margin of your Bible, record in as few words as possible what each division is about.

DAY FOUR

So often when calamity hits a nation people ask, "Why has this happened to us?" Let's begin our study today by seeing if the text gives a reason for the plague of locusts in the time of Joel.

Read Joel 2:12-14 and mark every reference to *the LORD* in a distinctive color or with a symbol. Don't miss the pronouns!

Now in the light of what you just read (which is God's Word to His covenant nation of Israel), what is God telling His people to do, and what does this imply?

According to Joel 1, the plague of locusts literally devoured everything edible, leaving not only the people but even the animals in a desperate state. Was this a judgment from God, an act of fate, or just "Mother Nature"? Look up the following verses and see what you learn. Record insights about locusts and/or plagues: Exodus 10:1-20; Deuteronomy 28:58-61; Isaiah 26:8-9; 45:6-7; Ezekiel 14:12-14; Amos 3:6; 4:6-12. (The Hebrew word translated "caterpillar" in Amos 4:9 is the same word translated "gnawing locust" in Joel 1:4).

DAY FIVE

Having established the reason for the plague of locusts, let's return to Joel 1 to solidify our understanding of several critical things that we saw in this chapter.

First, look at the call to wail in 1:8,11, and 13. What was the reason? *He said, this is your doing so they may go to him*

Look up the following verses and record what you learn from the text about the significance of grain and drink (libation) offerings. Remember to ask the 5 W's and an H.

- Genesis 35:14. This is the first use of "drink offering" in the Bible. Note the circumstances attending it. Note that Jacob did this long before the Law and the temple were parts of Israel's worship.

- Exodus 25:23-30. This passage contains instructions for furnishing the sanctuary—the tabernacle God commanded them to build that He might dwell with them. Note where they were to put the bowls for the drink offering.

- Exodus 29:38-42.

- Philippians 2:17 and 2 Timothy 4:6. The apostle Paul's metaphorical use of the drink offering is interesting.

Let's look at what we learn from marking *sackcloth*. God tells the priests and ministers of the altar to gird themselves with sackcloth. Why? What is its purpose? Look up the following passages and record what you learn about sackcloth: Genesis 37:34; Esther 4:1-3; Isaiah 15:1-3; Daniel 9:1-3; Jonah 3:4-10; Matthew 11:21; Revelation 6:12.

Joel also calls the leaders to declare a solemn assembly. What does Scripture tell us about such an assembly? Look up the following verses and see what you learn from them. Remember, examine them in their context, and note who, what, when, where, why and how: Leviticus 23:36; Numbers 29:35; Deuteronomy 16:8; 2 Kings 10:20; 2 Chronicles 7:9; Amos 5:21.

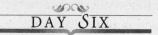

DAY SIX

God calls His people to consecrate a fast. Read the following scriptures to see what you can learn and put into practice. Note who fasts, what kind of a fast it is, why and when they fast, and what (if anything) accompanies the fast. Also note what happens as a result of the fast: 1 Samuel 7:3-14; 2 Samuel 1:12; 12:13-23; 1 Kings 21:20-29; Ezra 8:21-23; Nehemiah 1:1–2:8; Esther 4:13–5:3; Psalm 35:13; Isaiah 58:1-12; Jeremiah 14:10-12; Daniel 9:1-4; Zechariah 7:5-10; Matthew 6:1,16-18; Luke 5:30-35; Acts 13:1-3;14:23.

Record the theme of this first chapter on the JOEL AT A GLANCE chart on page 57.

DAY SEVEN

 Store in your heart: Joel 1:15
Read and discuss: Joel 1:13-20

QUESTIONS FOR DISCUSSION OR INDIVIDUAL STUDY

- What disaster occurred in Israel? Was it a "natural" disaster? *Supernatural Disaster God wants us to turn back to Him*
- Why did the plague of locusts occur? What was its purpose? *It was a sin against God, because of Isreal unfaithfullness*
- How was Israel to respond? *To be sad in their sins, to be ashamed*
- Discuss what you learned about sackcloth, fasting, and solemn assemblies. *The sackcloth was for mourning to show they were upset, Fasting- to turn from their wicked ways by praying and wearing rough cloths and called To God*

- If famine, drought, floods, earthquakes, and plagues come to our country, what's the first thing we should do? *Fast and pray*

- How does Joel 2:12-13 fit with the plague? What is the application for our lives? For your life? *Return to God- Stay close to the Lord*

- Has your church or ministry ever had a "solemn assembly" to mourn, fast, humble yourself, and cry out to God? What happened?

- Share what you learned about drink offerings. *Where He will meet with His people*

- Why are gladness and joy cut off from the house of the Lord when the priests cannot offer grain and drink offerings? *They are not meeting with God*

- What does this tell you about true worship? *He wants you to meet with Him*

- What does giving to the Lord have to do with the drink offering and worship? *Giving back what he has given you*

- What place does fasting have in the church today? What place *should* it have? *I think we should fast*

THOUGHT FOR THE WEEK

More than 2500 years ago, the people of Israel suffered an invasion of locusts that left them without food, wine, and oil. They and their animals were hungry; they had nothing to bring as offerings, and they were without joy in the house of the Lord.

Why does God cause such calamity? Perhaps this story will help us understand:

> In the early spring of 1877, Minnesota farmers surveyed their lands, dreading the first hordes of locusts that had caused such widespread

destruction the summer before. Another such plague threatened to destroy Minnesota's rich wheat lands, spelling ruin for thousands of families.

Suddenly Governor John S. Pillsbury proclaimed April 26 a day of fasting and prayer, urging that every man, woman, and child ask divine help. A strange hush fell over the land as Minnesotans solemnly assembled to pray. The next morning, the sun rose in cloudless skies. Temperatures soared to mid-summer heat. The people looked up at the skies in wonder, and to their horror, the warm earth began to stir with the dreaded insects.

This was a strange answer! Three days passed. The unseasonable heat hatched out a vast army of locusts that threatened to engulf the entire Midwest! Then, on the fourth day, the sun went down in a cold sky, and that night frost gripped the earth. Most of the locusts were destroyed as surely as if fire had swept them away! When summer came the wheat waved tall and green. April 26 went down in history as the day on which a people's prayer had been answered.*

The Minnesotans turned to God in the midst of the calamity of locusts. They sought God with prayer and fasting. Israel too was called to seek God. God designed their calamity to turn their attention back to the only One who could give them a second chance.

How simplistic we are about how things really work. We think we have solutions to our day-to-day problems. Something breaks or fails, and we start fixing it. We have a

---

* P.L. Tan, *Encyclopedia of 7700 Illustrations* (Garland, TX: Bible Communications, 1996).

problem, and we find a solution. We work harder or longer or both so we can keep business or ministry going as if they depended only on how hard we worked.

Then one day disaster strikes, and our work won't fix it; we can't solve the problem. No matter how hard or long we work, we can't overcome this particular situation. What is God trying to do? Doesn't He realize how frustrating this is? Doesn't He know how much disasters hurt physically and emotionally?

Yes, He does, and He wants us to proclaim a solemn assembly, to seek Him in sackcloth and fasting. Some problems are so huge we have to turn to Him. They reveal our spiritual poverty, our desperation, our complete and utter dependence on Him.

We need to believe, though, that if God uses this method to turn us back, we must have gone somewhere we shouldn't have gone and need turning back. We must need a second chance even if we don't realize it until the disaster strikes. We tend to become complacent in our self-sufficiency, trusting in our own strength, talents, and abilities.

Stressful situations prove to us that we need God. Think about it. If we had adequate income, rest, fulfilling careers, happy homes, good health, solid community relationships, no crime, no disease, no shortages, and world peace, how reliant on God would we be? Wouldn't Satan do all in his power to convince us we have created all these things? Wouldn't we fall prey to the idea that man can solve any problem? After all, isn't that what science and research claim? Don't we pay taxes for the government to solve all society's problems?

Where is God? The world doesn't care or wonder! Where do the perplexed, the persecuted, the downtrodden, the impoverished, the weak, the sick seek relief? Has any government formed by men found the answer? Communists trumpeted a system that would create utopia. It didn't. Capitalists crowed that their economic model and a democratic political system would provide a better life for all mankind. It hasn't.

No man-made institution will suffice. We need God. ("Blessed is the nation whose God is the LORD"—Psalm 33:12.) Even the chosen nation needs God. And God won't let us forget it, either. He always allows enough "stuff" in our lives to remind us that we are human, not divine. When we get too far away from Him, He allows some really big calamities to occur.

Secular society talks about "natural" disasters—floods, earthquakes, forest fires, plagues, locusts. But interestingly, insurance policies call such events "acts of God," meaning "supernatural," which is true. Even unbelievers know God is in charge of nature though they don't like giving Him credit.

One day the Lord will come back to earth to judge mankind. Men will be without excuse because everyone has knowledge of God through creation (see Romans 1:18-20) even if they refuse to acknowledge their Creator and choose to worship created things instead.

Great disasters will appear in the heavens and on earth before the Lord's return—when He comes, no one will mistake it. He isn't coming secretly in the form of a baby as He did the first time. He is coming in glory and power, and He will judge mankind. Those who have not believed will have missed their chance.

Everything that happens today in the realm of nature is only a foreshadowing of the great and terrible day of the Lord. God intends each foreshadowing to bring us back to Him, to give us a second chance. He intends each one to energize us, to impel us forward for His kingdom and to a position of total dependence on Him.

Prayer, fasting, sackcloth, and solemn assembly are expressions of that dependence. But should we consider them today? What should we do?

We should depend on God.

Week two in Joel

Blow a Trumpet in Zion

Is now the time to blow a trumpet, sound an alarm, consecrate a fast? Yes, oh yes. But who is willing?

Few today live in cities with stone walls surrounding and protecting them. Our cities don't have watchtowers, gates, or watchmen on walls ready to blow trumpets to sound alarms of impending danger. So what is the modern equivalent to this Old Testament function? How can we be watchmen on walls, ready to sound alarms, ready to blow trumpets? And if we can discover *how* from the Bible, are we willing?

DAY ONE

Read Joel 2, paying close attention to references to time, including words that indicate sequences of events. Make sure you mark words like *now, then, never again, after, in those days,* and *before.* A good way to mark time references is with a clock as we showed you on page 7 of "Getting Started."

Read Joel 2:1-17 again, this time marking the following key words and phrases, each in its own distinctive color or way: *the day of the Lord* (including synonyms), geographical locations (such as *Holy mountain*[3] and *Zion*), *the land* (when referring to the land God gave Israel [Jacob] and his sons as an everlasting possession), *the Lord, the nations, army,*[4] *fast* and *fasting, weep,* and *My Spirit.*

DAY TWO

Read Joel 2:18-32 today, marking the same key words and phrases as you did yesterday. When you finish, list what you learn from marking each one. You can do this on a separate piece of paper or in your notebook.

Now divide the text of Joel 2 into segments. Draw a line each time the topic seems to change.

DAY THREE

We need to identify whom or what the pronouns "them" and "their" in 2:3-10 refer to. Joel 1 mentioned a great locust plague. How does Joel 1:6 describe the locusts? How do they leave the land?

Read Joel 2:1-2. The inhabitants of the land are to tremble before whose coming?

Now read Joel 2:3-10. What does the description here sound like? Is it similar to the locust plague in Joel 1?

One interpretive issue is whether the army of people coming in Joel 2:3-10 *is* another locust plague like the one in Joel 1 or simply *like* the plague—a people foreshadowed by locusts. Commentators disagree, so how can we sort it out?

Read Joel 2:1-2 and 11 again and identify who is coming and when. Who opposes the advancing enemy?

In the context of Joel 2:18-20, God the Lord says, "I will never again make you a reproach among the nations. But I will remove the northern army far from you." According to the context, how were these people made a reproach?

Now let's stop and review what we have seen. Right from the beginning of his prophecy, Joel wants each generation to know what happened as a result of the great locust plague (Joel 1:2-3). It was a plague of such magnitude that it serves as a permanent reminder of the coming day of the Lord. Speaking of that day, God says, "There has never been anything like it, nor will there be again after it to the years of many generations" (Joel 2:2).

At this point, we think you will appreciate reading this article about locusts, having observed Joel 2:3-10. Read it through, watching for any parallels in Joel.

> There are ten Hebrew words used in Scripture to signify locust. In the New Testament locusts are mentioned as one of the foods of John the Baptist (Matt. 3:4; Mark 1:6). By Mosaic Law they were reckoned "clean," so John could lawfully eat them. The word also occurs in Rev. 9:3, 7, in allusion to this devastating Oriental insect.
>
> Locusts belong to the class of Orthoptera (i.e., straight-winged). There are many species. The ordinary Syrian locust resembles the grasshopper but it's larger and more destructive. "The legs and thighs of these insects are so powerful that they can leap to a height of two hundred times the length of their bodies. When so raised they spread their wings and fly so close together as to appear like one compact moving mass."

Locusts are prepared as food in various ways. Sometimes they are pounded, mixed with flour and water, then baked into cakes "sometimes boiled, roasted, or stewed in butter, and then eaten." They were preserved and eaten by the ancient Assyrians.

The devastations they make in Eastern lands are often appalling, among the worst calamities that can occur. "Their numbers exceed computation: the Hebrews called them 'the countless,' and the Arabs knew them as 'the darkeners of the sun.' Unable to guide their own flight, though capable of crossing large spaces, they are at the mercy of the wind, which bears them as blind instruments of Providence to the doomed region given over to them for the time. Innumerable as the drops of water or the sands of the seashore, their flight obscures the sun and casts a thick shadow on the earth (Exodus 10:15; Judges 6:5; 7:12; Jeremiah 46:23; Joel 2:10). It seems indeed as if a great aerial mountain, many miles in breadth, were advancing with a slow, unresting progress. Woe to the countries beneath them if the wind fall and let them alight! They descend unnumbered as flakes of snow and hide the ground. It may be 'like the garden of Eden before them, but behind them is a desolate wilderness. At their approach the people are in anguish; all faces lose their color' (Joel 2:6). No walls can stop them; no ditches arrest them; fires kindled in their path are forthwith extinguished by the myriads of their dead, and the countless armies march on (Joel 2:8, 9). If a door or a window be open, they enter and destroy everything of wood in the house. Every terrace, court, and inner chamber is filled with them in a moment. Such an awful visitation swept over Egypt (Ex. 10:1-19), consuming before it every green thing, and stripping the trees, till the land was bared of all signs of vegetation. A strong north-west wind from the Mediterranean swept the locusts into the Red Sea."*

Now read Revelation 9:1-11. Watch for the word *locusts* and note how they are described.

DAY FOUR

Read Joel 2:1-2 and then read Joel 2:15. What do these verses have in common?

Are the trumpets in Joel being sounded for the same purpose? Check the context of these verses and then record why the trumpets are blown. *NO one is a warning*

the second for a fast

The following scriptures will give you insight into God's ordinances regarding trumpets: Numbers 10:1-10; 29:1; 31:6. How does this compare to God's directions in Joel? In other words, was this a shock to the people or something they were familiar with? *they should be familiar*

In the light of the devastation of the locusts, the people are to blow a trumpet, warning the people of an even more disastrous time, the coming day of the Lord (2:1-2).

Yet, as you observed, God tells His people to blow a trumpet in Zion, consecrate a fast, and call the people, young and old, to a solemn assembly. If they respond to God's call, according to verse 17 what will they do? *weep*

Now, read Joel 2:18-27. What will the Lord do? What will happen to the land, the beasts, the weather, and the crops? And what will the people know? *the lord will restore their land. Forgive them. That god is in the midst of Israel*

* M.G. Easton, *Easton's Bible Dictionary* (Oak Harbor, WA: Logos Research Systems, 1996). Internal quotes are from Cunningham Geike, *Hours with the Bible* (New York: James Pott and Company, 1903).

Now, Beloved, record the theme of Joel 2 on JOEL AT A GLANCE on page 57.

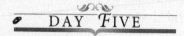

DAY FIVE

Today, simply observe Joel 3. Make sure you mark every time phrase and every reference to *the nations*,[5] including pronouns like *yourselves*. Double underline or mark every geographical location (including the countries mentioned) along the way. Mark every *I* or *I will* of the Lord. Mark every reference to *Israel*—you can use a star of David. Mark the reference to the *day of the LORD*.

As you do all this, notice how the text flows from the end of Joel 2 into Joel 3.

DAY SIX

Read through Joel 3 to put yourself back into context. Then record in your notebook or on a separate piece of paper what you learned by marking every *I* and every *I will*. Also list everything you learn from marking *nations*.

What do you learn about Israel? What do you learn from marking the references to Jerusalem, which Joel also refers to as Zion?

In Joel 3:9, God says, "Prepare a war," and then in verses 11-12, He speaks of the nations gathering in the valley of Jehoshaphat. How does Joel describe this valley?

Read Revelation 16:12-16 and note who is coming from where and why.

Now compare Joel 3 with Revelation 14:17-20 and Isaiah 34:6. Observe the location of the wine press. The marginal note in Revelation 14:20 says that "200 miles" is "1600 stadia" in the Greek, and that a stadia was about 600 feet. A little arithmetic tells us that 1600 stadia is almost 182 miles. The distance from Megiddo to Bozrah in Edom, present day Jordan, is about 176 miles. Do you see any correlation?

Finally, record the theme of Joel 3 on JOEL AT A GLANCE. Then determine the overall theme of Joel and record it on JOEL AT A GLANCE.

DAY SEVEN

 Store in your heart: Joel 2:12

Read and discuss: Joel 2:1-2,11-14; 3:1-2,9-17

QUESTIONS FOR DISCUSSION OR INDIVIDUAL STUDY

- ∽ Discuss the characteristics of the day of the Lord.

- ∽ What will happen to Israel in the day of the Lord? What will happen to the nations?

- ∽ What will happen *before* the day of the Lord?

- ∽ Discuss the valley of Jehoshaphat. What is its place in the day of the Lord?

- ∽ What is the purpose of the day of the Lord and the events in the valley of Jehoshaphat?

- What do we learn about God from what He says He will do in the day of the Lord?

- Now, from what you learn about God in Joel, what application can you make to your own life? For example, will God be just?

- Does knowing about the day of the Lord motivate you or affect your prayer life? For whom or what do you pray? Why?

THOUGHT FOR THE WEEK

"Multitudes, multitudes in the valley of decision." The day of the Lord will come with vengeance on the enemies of Israel and vindication for those who return to the Lord. The prophet Joel brought this message from the Lord to the kingdom of Judah almost 3000 years ago: "Return to me with all your heart."

A second chance is what Joel preached—a second chance to worship God, to obey His commandments. Oh, how we need that message today too! Our nations live in open defiance of God with perverted and debased morals—abominations in the sight of God. Murder of unborn children, pornography, fornication, and adultery abound. Those who speak out against these things are ridiculed, labeled narrow-minded, simpleminded, unrealistic busybodies. Some people say we cannot legislate morals, and they use freedom of expression, freedom of speech, and freedom of behavior to worship immorality.

Many believe the new religion of this century is sex. Its high priest is Hugh Hefner (the founder of *Playboy* magazine), and its temples are televisions, theaters, and the Internet.

But judgment is coming. Just as surely as Joel declared to Israel its need to return to God with fasting, sackcloth, and solemn assemblies, our nations need to repent as well. Judgment is coming, and no *nation* is exempt. And if *you* worship at the feet of the god of sex and do not live according to the precepts for life God gave us in His holy Word, then you will be judged too.

Joel's message held out the hope to Israel that if they returned to God (if revival broke out among them), He would withhold punishment. But He would judge the nations who oppressed Israel.

God is a just Judge. He does not let the guilty go unpunished. Those who oppress the people of God receive their just reward. Those who wag the finger in the face of those who say "Thus saith the Lord," those who laugh and ridicule, who curl the lip and turn their backs on God's Word will all suffer the consequences of their actions.

What should we do? Gloat over their judgment? Pray for them? Should we give in, or should we continue speaking the pure, unadulterated truth and blow the trumpet of warning in the face of ridicule?

Ezekiel 33:2-9 says this:

> Son of man, speak to the sons of your people and say to them, "If I bring a sword upon a land, and the people of the land take one man from among them and make him their watchman, and he sees the sword coming upon the land and blows on the trumpet and warns the people, then he who hears the sound of the trumpet and does not take warning, and a sword comes and takes him away, his blood will be on his own head. He heard the sound of the trumpet but did not take warning; his

blood will be on himself. But had he taken
warning, he would have delivered his life.
But if the watchman sees the sword coming
and does not blow the trumpet and the people
are not warned, and a sword comes and takes
a person from them, he is taken away in his
iniquity; but his blood I will require from the
watchman's hand."

Now as for you, son of man, I have
appointed you a watchman for the house of
Israel; so you will hear a message from My
mouth and give them warning from Me. When
I say to the wicked, "O wicked man, you will
surely die," and you do not speak to warn the
wicked from his way, that wicked man shall die
in his iniquity, but his blood I will require from
your hand. But if you on your part warn a
wicked man to turn from his way and he does
not turn from his way, he will die in his iniquity, but you have delivered your life.

Are you a watchman, Beloved? Will you blow the
trumpet?

I Will Pour Out My Spirit on All Mankind

❧❧❧❧

" 'Not by might, nor by power, but by My Spirit' says the Lord of Hosts." Can the Spirit of the Lord help us escape the wrath and judgment to come, when there will be "multitudes in the valley of decision"?

DAY ONE

Last week we observed Joel 2–3. This week, let's go back to Joel 2:28-32, which contains a jaw-dropping promise. In the days of Joel, only priests, prophets, and kings experienced the pouring out of the Spirit. Now here is a promise that goes far beyond them.

What is the promise? When will it come? Can we find any time indicators that reveal when God will fulfill this promise?

Only one other book in the Bible refers to Joel by name—the book of Acts. Read Acts 2:1-39. Where does it mention Joel?

When do these events occur?

Read Acts 2:1-39 again and mark every reference to the *Spirit,*[6] *promise, the day of the Lord, repent,* and all time phrases.

DAY TWO

Let's move on in Acts to about eight years after Pentecost. In a vision, God told Cornelius, a Gentile centurion living in Caesarea under the authority of Rome, to send for the apostle Peter.

Read Acts 10:44-48 and note what happens when he hears the message that Jesus died for his sins and then rose from the dead. Observe how Peter explains this to his Jewish brethren in Christ.

Read Acts 11:12-18 and note the conclusion of the Jewish brethren in verse 18 and how it goes with Acts 2:39.

Look up the following verses, which shed even more light on this "outpouring of God's Holy Spirit" or "the gift of the Spirit." As you read these passages, mark references to the *Holy Spirit:* Ezekiel 36:22-28; Romans 8:11-14,16; Ephesians 1:13-14.

DAY THREE

Let's go back to Joel 2:28-32 one more time and look at the events that precede the day of the Lord.

According to these verses, what will precede the day of the Lord? (Remember, this was also recorded in Acts 2.)

In our study of Obadiah, you took a good look at scriptures that referred to the day of the Lord and recorded them on a chart on pages 26–27. Now add your insights from Joel to this chart. (Go back to every reference you marked in Joel and record that information on the chart.)

DAY FOUR

You may have noticed yesterday that one scripture said a *remnant* of Israel would be saved in the day of God's wrath. Read Joel 2:32 very carefully. According to this verse, who will escape? *Who ever calls on the name of the Lord*

Now let's cross-reference Joel 2:32 with the following verses. Look them up and note what you learn about the remnant even though the word is not always used. As you do, remember that if Joel was written at an early date as many believe, then all the prophets you are about to look up arrive on the scene after Joel: Isaiah 10:20-23; Daniel 12:1; Zechariah 13:8-9

When you parallel Joel 2:1-2 and Daniel 12:1 with Matthew 24:21 you'll see an interesting connection. Look at those three verses and see what they have in common. Do you think the great tribulation is synonymous with the day of the Lord?

Read Matthew 24:15-31. Starting in verse 15, circle the word *when* and then connect it with a line to the next *then*. Circle the *then* and do the same through verse 29, connecting the words that give you a sequence of time. Include "immediately after the tribulation of those days" (verse 29) in the line connection between verse 23 and 30. See what you get. Also mark the word *tribulation*[7] and put a cloud around any reference to the coming of the Son of Man—that's Jesus! He's the One speaking in this passage. Again He's letting them know He is the Son of Man Daniel described (Daniel 7), who will return in power and glory and set up His throne! Remember, you are looking for clues to what happens to the remnant (the elect), so mark *elect*.

Finally, dear student of the Word, read Jeremiah 30:1-11. Notice the reference to "that day" in verse 7, what will happen to "Jacob" (Israel) then, and the reason why—given in the final verses of this passage.

DAY FIVE

Yesterday we looked at Matthew 24 and the events leading up to the coming of the Lord on the clouds of the sky with power and great glory. Now what happens next?

Read Matthew 24:15-31 again. Jesus gathers His elect from the four winds—in other words, from every corner of the earth. And then?

When Jesus comes back, where does He come to? Read the following and record your insights in your notebook: Joel 3:11-18; Zechariah 14:1-11 (watch the references to "in that day"); Revelation 19:11-21.

DAY SIX

When Jesus sits on His throne in Jerusalem, what does He do? Read Matthew 25:31-46. Mark every reference to Jesus, including all synonyms. Use a cloud to mark His coming. Mark references to *the nations*. Mark references to *the kingdom* and *eternal life* one way, and *eternal*[8] *punishment* another way (perhaps with red flames!).

On what basis are the righteous blessed?

Well, Beloved, after studying Joel, where do you think this judgment of the "sheep and the goats" takes place?

DAY SEVEN

 Store in your heart: Joel 3:12

Read and discuss: Joel 2:28-32; Matthew 24:29-31; Acts 2:38

QUESTIONS FOR DISCUSSION OR INDIVIDUAL STUDY

- Who are the recipients of the prophetic promise in Joel and Acts? Was this promise of the Holy Spirit only for the Jews? *on all mankind* *No* *whom ever calls on the name of the Lord. Jews + Gentiles*
- On whom would God pour out His Spirit? How does Joel describe this? *Before the Great an Glorious day of the Lord will be delivered*
- According to Joel, when would God fulfill this promise? According to Peter, when did this happen? *Before the day of the Lord*
- According to Joel and Acts, who is going to be saved? *whom ever calls on the name of the Lord*
- Can you see the application of the promise in Joel 2:28 to your own life? How? *when*

- Discuss the judgment of the sheep and the goats.

- What does this tell you about the importance of the way we treat "Jesus' brothers"?

∿ In all probability, you will not be involved in that judgment (except to be watching), for once the Lord comes for His own, we will ever be with Him. However, how does this promise apply to our relationships? *We will all be together in heaven*

∿ How does this impact your worldview, Beloved?
There are a lot of lost children

THOUGHT FOR THE WEEK

Now, faithful student, do what the Scriptures tell us to do: Examine yourself to see if you are in the faith (2 Corinthians 13:5). Does God's Spirit bear witness with your spirit that you are a child of God? Do you have a religion but not a relationship? Have you been learning much about God and about His Son, but Christ is not yet in you? If this is the case, turn to Romans 10:13, which quotes the last line of Joel's prophecy. Read Romans 10:8-13 slowly and carefully. According to verse 9, what must you do to be saved— to receive the gift of the Holy Spirit, which is synonymous with salvation?

If God has spoken to your heart, and this is the day of your salvation, Beloved of God, then do what Romans 10:9 says.

Write out below the words as you say them, and you'll have a record of this momentous occasion when you moved from death to life, from the power of Satan to the kingdom of God, when you received forgiveness of sins and became an heir of God, a joint heir with Jesus Christ. Put down the date, and then, if you would, share it with us. We would like to send you a special gift in celebration of your new birth. Welcome to God's forever family, Beloved.

Theme of Joel:

SEGMENT DIVISIONS

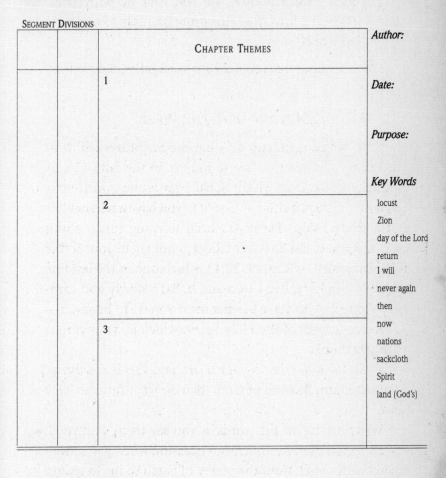

		CHAPTER THEMES
		1
		2
		3

Author:

Date:

Purpose:

Key Words

locust

Zion

day of the Lord

return

I will

never again

then

now

nations

sackcloth

Spirit

land (God's)

Amos

INTRODUCTION TO AMOS

Once again God speaks through yet another prophet, a prophet whose message will endure throughout time, whose words will not pass away until all is fulfilled (Matthew 5:17-18). How critical it is, then, that we study his prophecy and order our lives accordingly.

Unlike Obadiah and Joel, we know when Amos lived and prophesied. Amos was a prophet to the northern kingdom, Israel, but his message included other nations. Thus the principles from his message apply to anyone willing to read, hear, and listen to the Word of God.

Like Obadiah and Joel, Amos brings a message that is designed to spark a change in Israel's behavior and attitude toward God, to give them a second chance. The northern kingdom had strayed to idol worship immediately after Solomon died, and now, 160 years later, they still worshipped golden calves and the gods of the nations around them. God called them to return to Him, and He used an ordinary man—Amos.

THE LORD HAS ROARED FROM ZION

Who will listen and fear? Who will listen and live accordingly? Who will listen?

DAY ONE

Read through the book of Amos in one sitting. This will help you familiarize yourself with the basic content of the book. Every time you come to *thus says the Lord,*[1] *hear this word the Lord has spoken,*[2] *declares the Lord,*[3] *the Lord has sworn*—any phrase that indicates the Lord speaking—color-code it.

DAY TWO

Today, read through Amos again. This time watch for references (people and events) that give you the historical context of the book. Watch for natural divisions in this book. You can see them by marking the following: *Hear the word which the* LORD *has spoken, hear this word, thus the Lord* GOD *showed me,*[4] and *I saw the* LORD.

You can note these references in your notebook or put them on the AMOS AT A GLANCE chart on page 111.

DAY THREE

What did you learn about Amos from chapter one? Look for his home town on the map THUS SAYS THE LORD TO...on page 63. Also consult the historical chart THE RULERS AND PROPHETS OF AMOS'S TIME on page 63 to see the relationships between these kings and Amos.

To better appreciate the times and God's Word through Amos, let's go to Kings and Chronicles to find out what we can about these men. Because we have more to read in connection with Uzziah, let's look at Jeroboam first.

Read 2 Kings 14:23-29. As you read, observe Jeroboam's genealogy because another Jeroboam preceded him.

In your notebook, note what you learn about Jeroboam II and about the times.

Now let's turn our attention to the reign of Uzziah. Read 2 Kings 15:1-7. Uzziah is called Azariah in 2 Kings, but Chronicles and Isaiah call him Uzziah. Note his genealogy and what the religious climate was like for Judah, the southern kingdom, under his reign.

Second Chronicles 25:27–26:23 gives us an account of Uzziah's reign and how he came to the throne. Note Judah's prosperity and military power under Uzziah's reign.

Even though Uzziah did what was right by the Lord, he did not encourage the people in high places to do so.

God places people around us who can benefit from our influence.

Thus Says the Lord to...

~~~~~~

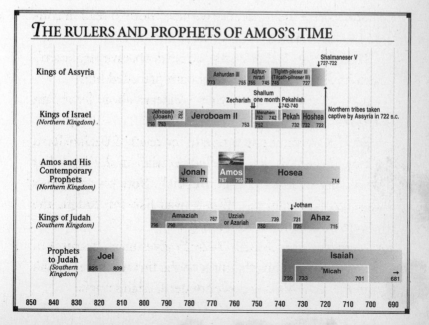

THE RULERS AND PROPHETS OF AMOS'S TIME

The chart spans years 850 B.C. to 690 B.C.

Kings of Assyria
- Ashurdan III (773–755)
- Ashur-nirari (755–745)
- Tiglath-pileser III (Tiglath-pilneser III) (745–727)
- Shalmaneser V (727–722)

Kings of Israel (Northern Kingdom)
- Jehoash (Joash) (798–793)
- Jeroboam II (793–753)
- Zechariah (753–752)
- Shallum one month (752)
- Menahem (752–742)
- Pekahiah (742–740)
- Pekah (742–732)
- Hoshea (732–722)
- Northern tribes taken captive by Assyria in 722 B.C.

Amos and His Contemporary Prophets (Northern Kingdom)
- Jonah (784–772)
- Amos (767–755)
- Hosea (755–714)

Kings of Judah (Southern Kingdom)
- Amaziah (796–767)
- Uzziah or Azariah (790–739)
- Jotham (750–731)
- Ahaz (735–715)

Prophets to Judah (Southern Kingdom)
- Joel (825–809)
- Isaiah (739–681)
- Micah (733–701)

DAY FOUR

Now let's go to the prophet Isaiah, whose opening chapters give us a sense of the moral and spiritual temperature of the two kingdoms during the reigns of Jeroboam II and Uzziah. Note the timing of Isaiah's prophecy by reading Isaiah 1:1 and 6:1.

Then read Isaiah 1 and watch for references to the nation's spiritual condition. If you have a pencil, you may want to underline those references.

Note how God describes Himself and what He calls the people to do.

Now read Isaiah 5:7-25 very carefully. Make three headings as shown below in your notebook, and note what you learn about the economic, moral, and spiritual status of the nation at that time.

ECONOMIC   MORAL   SPIRITUAL

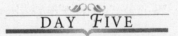

DAY FIVE

Amos 1–2 is a unit, but we'll break up our time observing these two chapters. Today, we'll look only at Amos 1.

Amos is 9 chapters long, so you might want to make a bookmark with key words and phrases you will mark in more than one or two chapters.

Marking time phrases and geographical locations is important. Also mark countries that Amos mentions. As you do, look them up on the map on page 63 so you understand where they are relative to the northern and southern kingdoms.

Mark the key repeated phrase *for three transgressions*[5] *of…and for four* in these first two chapters by highlighting, shading, or underlining.

As you read through Amos 1, did you see a pattern in the content of each message? If so, what is it?

The Hebrew word translated "transgressions"[6] here in Amos is transliterated* *peshah. Peshah* generally means "sins" but specifically "rebellion against authority." In this case, it is rejection or rebellion against God's authority.

DAY SIX

Amos 1 mentions five nations whose transgressions the Lord will punish. Thoroughly developing the biblical background of each to understand who they were, what their relationship to Israel was, and why the Lord wanted to punish them is a lot more work than we have time for in this Bible study, so we will give you just a couple of references to look up.

Read the following scriptures and record your insights about each country in your notebook:

Damascus/Aram—Genesis 10:1,22; 25:20; 2 Kings 13:1-5; Isaiah 7:8.

Gaza/Philistines—Genesis 10:6-14; Joshua 13:1-3; Judges 10:6-7; 13:1; 1 Samuel 4:1-2; 7:3-14; 17:1-4.

---

* The transliteration is the spelling in English letters that gives the sounds of the letters in the original language, such as Hebrew or Greek.

Tyre—2 Samuel 5:11; 1 Kings 5:1; Psalm 83:1-7; Jeremiah 47:4; Ezekiel 26:2-7; Joel 3:4-6.

Edom—If you have already studied Obadiah, simply review those parts of the lesson that speak of Edom. If not, you'll need to look up these verses and summarize what you learn about Edom: Genesis 25:20-34; 27:41; 28:6-9; Numbers 20:21; Deuteronomy 2:1-5,12; 1 Kings 11:14-17; 22:47; 2 Kings 8:20; Hebrews 12:15-17.

Ammon—Genesis 19:30-38; Deuteronomy 2:19; Judges 3:12-13; 10:6-9; 1 Kings 11:7; Zephaniah 2:8. Some of the verses that describe Ammon's relationship to Israel will also tell you about Moab's relationship, so make note of both.

Now summarize the theme or message of Amos 1 and record it on AMOS AT A GLANCE on page 111.

DAY SEVEN

 Store in your heart: Amos 1:2

Read and discuss: Amos 1

QUESTIONS FOR DISCUSSION OR INDIVIDUAL STUDY

ᐁ Discuss the background (setting) of Amos. What was going on in Israel?

ᐁ Discuss each of the five nations the Lord sent fire upon. Who were they, and what were their relationships to Israel? What were their transgressions?

- ✎ Do these relationships have an application today? Are any nations approaching Israel to destroy it? Have any of these nations attacked Israel in the last 50 years?

- ✎ Discuss the spiritual condition of Israel. Does this parallel the situation in your country today?

- ✎ What should you do in your country? Should you speak out? How?

THOUGHT FOR THE WEEK

The Lord roars from Zion. He roars justice. The neighboring nations had one thing in common: They did not treat Israel as the special, chosen people of the one true God. Why not? Partly because they did not acknowledge God. They had their own gods. This is very much like our world today. People do not acknowledge the God of the Bible as *the* God—Father, Son, and Spirit. Because they do not acknowledge the God of the Bible, they do not treat His people well. They can't imagine that their god is inferior, that their religion is not the right one.

They insist on tolerance for their religions while demanding that others be silenced. They plan against God's people to destroy them, but God will render justice even though His people are persecuted today. Persecution is a normal part of Christianity. Second Timothy 3:12 tells us that "all who desire to live godly in Christ Jesus will be persecuted." The "will be" means that persecution is certain. If God had meant it was uncertain, that it only *might* happen, the English would read that way.

Acts records the persecutions of Christians at the hands of Jews and Greeks. Paul wrote about many persecutions he endured, and he mentions that the Lord delivered him out of them all. That's really the key, Beloved—the Lord will deliver us from our persecutors.

Amos prophesies the destruction of those who persecuted the Jews in the promised land. His message and the New Testament inform us that the Lord will also destroy those who persecute us. But as you study Amos, you'll see that Israel and Judah are not exempt from judgment, and neither are we.

God promises to purify His saints with trials, tribulations, and persecutions. He will rescue us, but He uses these pressures to refine us like silver, to purify and cleanse us so that we will be holy and blameless before Him. God intends to test and prove His servants in this life so that we will stand before Him for eternity in the fullness of the image of Christ.

But even as we stand before the judgment seat of Christ with the books opened to view the deeds we have done in the body, Christ will only judge us for reward or loss of reward—for what we might cast before the throne at the feet of Jesus. Our entrance to heaven is secured by the forgiveness of our sins—our redemption from sin by the blood of Christ. Our faith in the gospel assures us of that.

God who was, who is, and who is to come is the same yesterday, today, and forever. He does not change. The promises He made 3000 years ago still stand. The prophecies declared by His holy servants still stand and come true.

That's why we have hope when we read in Revelation 6:9-11 of the believers' cry for vengeance on those who had slain them, and see the Lord's promise that it will happen when the number slain is complete. Because Revelation declares victory—judgment on Satan and those belonging to his kingdom—we have hope. We have hope because the day of the Lord is coming, and on that day justice will prevail.

JUDGMENT BEGINS
IN THE
HOUSEHOLD OF GOD

Hearing Amos's pronouncement of judgment on the enemies of Israel is one thing; hearing that Israel is the "apple of [God's] eye" is another thing entirely! But the apple had some bad spots; decay had set in. And that was the problem.

DAY ONE

Today read through Amos 2 and mark the key repeated words and phrases from your bookmark. Again, note the nations Amos mentions and look them up on the map THUS SAYS THE LORD TO…on page 63.

Also, look for the same pattern in each message that you saw in Amos 1.

DAY TWO

The last of the nations that came against Israel is Moab—the brother of Ammon. As we did last week, let's look at this nation to see its relationship to Israel.

You saw that many of the scriptures that mentioned Ammon also mentioned Moab, so the following will not repeat any of those. These are just about Moab: Numbers 22:1-6; 25:1-2; Deuteronomy 2:9; 2 Chronicles 20:10-11.

A shift occurs between Amos 2:3 and 2:4. What is it?

Read Amos 2:4-5 and answer the 5 W's and an H from the text. For example: Who is speaking to whom? Why and what about? What is the issue? What are the consequences? How is God going to deal with the situation?

Why is Judah coming under the judgment of God? Did God rebuke and punish any of the other nations for this reason? If so, why?

Read 1 Peter 4:17. How does it relate?

The Hebrew word translated "lies"[7] in Amos 2:4 is *kazab,* which can also be translated "deception" or that which is not true, stressing the *act* of lying. Read Numbers 23:19; 2 Samuel 7:28; John 8:44; and John 17:14-19. What is the relationship between lies and false gods?

To understand why judgment is appropriate for Judah, read the following verses: Deuteronomy 8:19; 11:16; Habakkuk 2:18; Romans 1:20-25.

DAY THREE

Read Amos 2:6-16. This is the longest of the "thus says the Lord" messages. Do you see a change of direction in the message? What happens in verses 9-12? In 13-16?

Look at the description of Israel's sin in verses 6-8. In what ways was their sin apparent?

Remember the lawyer who challenged Jesus and Jesus' response to him? Read Matthew 22:35-40. Note the basis of the Law and how Jesus sums it up.

How were the Israelites in Amos's day breaking the Law?

In 2:9-12, God rehearses all He did for Israel, including raising up prophets and Nazirites.

Read Numbers 6:1-12 and see what you learn about Nazirites. How did Israel dishonor the Nazirites?

Now read Amos 2:13-16. According to verse 13, what had their sin done to God? What were the consequences of their sin?

Why do you think God uses the illustrations in verses 14-16? What does He want His people to understand?

DAY FOUR

Read Amos 3:1 and then look for the pattern of the messages to the various people groups in Amos 1–2. What happens in Amos 3? What indicates that this message is different from the ones in the first two chapters?

Now read Amos 3 and mark every reference to *Israel, iniquity,*[8] *transgression,*[9] and every reference to geographical locations.

When God addresses Israel in this chapter, is He talking to the northern kingdom, whose capital is Samaria, or to the whole kingdom of Israel—north and south? Give the reason for your answer from the text.

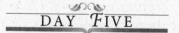

DAY FIVE

What do you learn about Israel's relationship to God and the responsibility that goes with it? Compare Exodus 19:3-6 with Amos 3.

Now read Ephesians 1:3-6. What should our attitude toward iniquity be?

The Hebrew word translated "chosen" in 3:2 is *yada*, meaning "known." In this context, it implies a relationship—knowledge that is intimate and not speculative (as in Abraham "knew" his wife). "Iniquity" is the translation of the Hebrew word *avon*, which refers to perverting or twisting the Law. It differs from "transgression," which means "rebellion against authority."

With this background, think about Amos 3:3-6 and what God is doing. What is God trying to show His elect people with each of these illustrations? Is the seriousness of each situation the same or different? What does God lead up to at the end of verse 6? What does He say in verse 7?

What is God letting Israel know? Why?

Does Amos 3:8 strike a familiar chord? Look at Amos 1:2, and then look up the following verses, noting how God describes Himself, to whom, and why: Hosea 5:8-14 (Ephraim is another name for Israel); 13:4-9.

Now, if the Lion, the Lord, has roared, according to verse 8 what will happen? What must Amos do?

DAY SIX

Now read Amos 3:9-15 and note what God tells the people to proclaim, where, and why. See what you learn from marking *Israel*.

What part of the nation of Israel is Amos 3:9-15 addressing? How do you know? Who is going to be snatched away?

Bethel had been a holy place from the time of Abraham. Read the following passages to gain an appreciation for this city: Genesis 12:8–13:4; 28:10-19; 35:1-7; 1 Kings 12:25-33. (*Beth* in Hebrew means "house" and *El* means "God," so *Bethel* means "house of God.")

What do you learn about the houses in the northern kingdom? Is Israel prosperous? How does their fate relate to Amos 1:1? What will happen in two years?

What did you learn about "natural" disasters from studying Joel? How does this fit with Numbers 32:23?

As your last assignment this week, determine the themes of Amos 2 and 3, and record them on AMOS AT A GLANCE on page 111.

DAY SEVEN

 Store in your heart: Amos 3:7

Read and discuss: Amos 3; 4:11-13

QUESTIONS FOR DISCUSSION OR INDIVIDUAL STUDY

- ∾ Compare the conditions in Amos's day to those in our day.

- ∾ What application to the church can we make from God's message to Israel?

- ∾ What does Peter mean when he says, "It is time for judgment to begin with the household of God"?

- The end of Amos 2:4 mentions the way "their fathers" walked. What does this tell you about the effect of one generation on another?

- Discuss the morals and mores* of your society. Is your society in trouble?

- What will break the cycle of sin? What will happen if it's not broken?

- Where do you think your generation and your children's generation are headed?

- If New Covenant believers, who have the Holy Spirit to empower them to obey God, are guilty of the same sins the Lord complained about to Israel, should they expect God's blessing or His chastening?

- Discuss Amos's description of the role of a prophet.

- What is your role as one who has the Word and Spirit of God? Can you keep silent? Or must you prepare people to meet *your* God?

- Now, Beloved, what are you going to do if God chastens you? What lesson have you learned?

THOUGHT FOR THE WEEK

Have you ever seen a billboard with these words on it in black and white?

PREPARE TO MEET YOUR GOD!

Did you wonder where those words came from? Did you think they originated with some zealous Christian or

---

* Mores (pronounced more-ays) are the customs and/or manners that prevail within groups, including social, religious, ethnic, and political groups. They define what the group or people hold to be right, acceptable, and obligatory.

religious fanatic? What did you think when you first saw them? Did you pray for all those who read their bold message? Or did they seem a little brazen, a little out of place on a roadside sign?

Now look around you. Mentally survey the morals and mores of your nation. For many of us, our countries once feared God, but they have now generally lost respect for Him and for His Word. Many of those who profess Christ have done the same.

Many churchgoers (not all) just want a quick fix from their Bible studies and sermons—which happen to be taught by people who are equally messed up but willing to share their stories without challenging the listeners to think, reason, or work their way through the Bible. That's too hard, and besides, life is too busy. They don't have time. They only want someone to relate to who will tell them in an entertaining way what to do and how to get out of the mess they're in.

Some say we will soon have a generation *subject* to lies—it won't even *recognize* them! You know what, faithful one? We already have that generation! We must stem *this* tide, turn *this* generation around, and lay a foundation for the *next* generation. This is why you must in turn convince others to study God's Word for themselves.

Winston Churchill, prime minister of Great Britain during World War II, wrote, "I was not the lion, but it fell to me to give the lion's roar." Oh, Beloved, you are not God, you are not the Savior, but it has fallen to you by virtue of your calling and intimate relationship with God—as His child, as a member of the body of Christ—to give the Lion's roar.

Are you prepared, Beloved? You surely want to be everything He wants you to be (including a workman who is not ashamed) because you are learning to handle His Word accurately.

We must speak out against the things God abhors. But we have to know God in order to know what God hates, what the abominations to Him are.

If we don't, judgment begins with the house of God. Those who know truth are accountable for truth. We can't hide from truth to avoid being accountable. If we have the means to learn truth, and we sit idly by, we are accountable for not acquiring truth. We're accountable either way.

An analogy from the world of team sports fits well here. Everyone in the body of Christ is "first string." Our team has no benchwarmers. No one gets to sit on the sideline and watch others play. Every team member belongs on the field, in the action!

You may object, "I don't have the spiritual gifts of teaching or prophecy!" This is no excuse. Those gifts may affect *how* you roar the Lion's roar but not *whether* you roar. Each of us has the ability to speak truth whenever and wherever we are confronted with lies. You may not have a platform for reaching thousands, but you can reach out to those God puts in your life as long as you're in this life.

If we rely on the "big name" speakers, writers, and radio and television personalities to do the roaring, we're depending on *them* to reach people who may never turn on the programs or read the Christian books. Where will they find truth? They live next door to you. They work with you. Their kids play sports with your kids.

You may think, *I don't know how to roar.* Share the Word of God. Share Jesus, who is coming back. The Word of God is complete—everything you and I need to know about God, man, and the future is there, Beloved, for you to discover through the discipline of study. This opportunity ought to not only thrill your heart but make you determined that you will spend the rest of your life poring over this Word so that you'll be able to intelligently warn others to flee from the wrath that is coming to test all those who dwell on the earth.

Roar the Lion's roar, but feed on the Lion's food first!

RETURN TO ME

Israel abandoned the Lord. They worshipped golden calves in Bethel and Dan, sacrificed on altars to Baal and on high places, and built idols, altars, and other things connected with the worship of the gods of the Gentiles. God didn't send fire from heaven to consume them all. He didn't send an invading army to destroy every man, woman, and child in Israel. That would have been just, but God wanted Israel and the world to know that He was a God of second chances. He wanted to give them a chance to return to Him. So he sent the shepherd, Amos, with a message.

DAY ONE

Now let's press on to Amos 4, which contains another word to hear from the Lord. Read Amos 4 and mark the same key words as before. This time, however, add the phrase *yet you have not returned to Me*. Also, locate the geographical references on the map on page 63.

What did you learn about God? What can He do? Read Amos 4 again, mark references to God, and list what you learned.

DAY TWO

What did you learn about the hearers in 4:1-3? What is going to happen and why?

Who are these "cows[10] of Bashan?" What wife would demand from her husband, "Bring now, that we may drink"?

Bashan is east of the Sea of Galilee, and Samaria is southwest. To understand why these women are called cows of Bashan even though they are on the Mount of Samaria, think about the times of the prophecy. Then read Jeremiah 50:19; Ezekiel 39:18; and Micah 7:14.

Women hold a vital role in God's economy. They are the backbones, supporting the heads, holding the families in place, and providing nurturing shelter for the next generation. Read 2 Timothy 3:1-7. Look at Paul's description of the character of people in the last days. Record in your notebook what you learn about "weak women."

Read Deuteronomy 15:11; 24:14; and Proverbs 14:31. What does the relationship these women—these cows of Bashan—had with the poor say about the relationship they had with God?

Now read Proverbs 31:10-31. What does a "Proverbs 31 woman" do for the poor and needy?

DAY THREE

Let's leave the women on the mountain of Samaria and move to Gilgal. Look up the following passages and record what you learn about Gilgal: Deuteronomy 11:29-32; Joshua 4:19-24; 5:10-12; 1 Samuel 11:15; Hosea 4:11-15; Amos 5:5.

(Hosea also prophesies during the reigns of Uzziah and Jeroboam II.)

Were the children of Israel still worshiping God, or had they turned away from their religious practices? Answer the question from the text.

What did God want from His people? Read Micah 6:6-8.

Why did God do what He did in Amos 4:6-11? In your notebook, make two lists like this:

WARNING   JUDGMENT

List warnings and judgments, beginning with "cleanness of teeth" (which implies famine) in verse 6 and going right through 4:11.

Now read Leviticus 26:17-33,40-46. Next to each judgment on your list, write the corresponding verse from Leviticus 26. (You can also do this with Deuteronomy 26, but that isn't necessary.)

Now, let's think this through. What have you just learned about God's judgments on His own, His children? What was their purpose, and what does this tell you about God?

What does God say His name is, and what is He implying by appealing to this particular name?

Finally, Beloved, what does God tell Israel to do in Amos 4:12?

DAY FOUR

Amos 5 begins another message from the Lord through Amos—exhortation, words of warning, and the prediction of exile.

Today, observe Amos 5:1-15 prayerfully. Add *remnant* to your bookmark, and be sure to mark other key words and phrases from your bookmark. Watch for the repeated plea to *live* and mark it. You will also see the word *hate*—which you can mark with a black heart.

Give careful attention to God as Amos takes up a dirge in chapter 5. Mark *God* in verses 8 and 9. What did you learn?

DAY FIVE

List in your notebook what you learn about Israel, Gilgal, Bethel, and the house of Joseph (Manasseh and Ephraim) from the dirge in Amos 5.

Apart from what is going to happen to Gilgal and Bethel, why does God tell them not to "resort" to Bethel and Gilgal? Why would they come to these places?

Read Amos 5:7. What does this verse tell you about justice in those days? Compare this with Habakkuk's burden in Habakkuk 1:1-4.

Where should Israel seek justice? Look at every place you marked *seek…that you may live.*

According to Amos, is everyone overcome by sin? Does everyone transgress? Are all unrighteous? What does the text tell you?

DAY SIX

We'll continue Amos 5 next week because we don't want to rush our study of this chapter. Today, just review what you've studied this week and catch up if you're behind.

Remember to determine the theme of Amos 4 and add it to your AMOS AT A GLANCE chart. By the way, if you're wondering what "segment divisions" are, they are groupings of chapters with common topics or styles. For example, the key repeated phrase *for three transgressions and four* appears in certain chapters (which ones?). This is the first segment. Then the subject changes (where?). This is the second segment. By the time you finish Amos, you will see three segments. To mark them on the chart, put a horizontal line where the divisions are and then write what the segment is about in the space provided.

DAY SEVEN

 Store in your heart: Amos 4:11

Read and discuss: Proverbs 31:20; Amos 4; 2 Timothy 3:1-7

QUESTIONS FOR DISCUSSION OR INDIVIDUAL STUDY

∾ Discuss the "cows of Bashan" and their rebellion.

∾ Contrast the "Proverbs 31 woman" with the women of 2 Timothy 3.

∾ Women, how do you measure up to biblical standards? Men, how can you help your wife be a "Proverbs 31 woman"?

∾ Why was sacrificing in Bethel or Gilgal a transgression?

∾ How does this relate to the way we worship? Do we worship as God instructs us—in spirit and truth?

∾ What did God do in the "natural" realm to get Israel to return to Him? Does Joel contain parallel teachings?

∾ When you see "natural" disasters in the world, do you interpret them as God's intention to turn men to Him?

∾ What did you learn about God in Amos 4? What does He do, and why does He do it?

∾ How should you respond to this message? How does the phrase "yet you have not returned to Me!" apply to you? Has God used any circumstances of your life to help you return to Him?

THOUGHT FOR THE WEEK

God frequently says "Return to Me" through His prophets. We saw the invitation in Joel and we see it again here in Amos. And we'll find it in Isaiah, Jeremiah, Hosea, Zechariah, and Malachi as well. Why does God repeat this message so much? Why does He send prophets to give people second chances? Why not just destroy all the wicked as He did in Noah's day?

The answer is that God is loving, merciful, compassionate, longsuffering, and covenant-keeping. God made a covenant with Israel to be their God. To be their God, He had to display His entire character, not just one aspect. He is just and holy and righteous, and therefore He must judge sin. He sent oppressors and plagues upon Israel. He used man and nature to help Israel see the error of their ways. He sent prophets to remind them what He had said about right and wrong, obedience and disobedience, blessing and curse. He was faithful to His character in all this.

But He was also faithful to His character to be a long-suffering and patient God of second chances. God did not create men to destroy them but to enjoy them. God wanted one creature to reflect His nature, and from the time that man sinned (rebelling, transgressing, and committing iniquity), God has been using man and nature to bring man back to Himself.

The day Adam sinned, he died. Since that time, God has orchestrated events to revive man, to give him a second chance at life. He promised a seed that had not come by the time of Amos but would surely come. Faith in that seed would bring righteousness and peace with God.

God sent prophet after prophet to announce this seed. He sent prophet after prophet to tell man that he was a sinner who needed to return to God. Some think that "Return to Me" means simply to return to obedience to God's Law. That's certainly part of the message to Israel, but it's not the whole message. The full message included having faith in God, trusting Him, and taking Him at His word. If people believed God for their redemption, He would accomplish it; they would receive mercy for their sins, and He would give the justice due those who oppressed them.

The answer was not in idols made with human hands—idols of wood, stone, silver, and gold. The answer was not in worshipping idols as if these gods *could* love them or do something for them. The answer is to take God at His word. That would actually be revival. And though Israel had strayed from Him, God would give them that second chance.

So it is today. God calls us to return to Him. If we are oblivious to God and His world around us, we will not hear the call. We must recognize that the God who calls us to fellowship with Him created and controls the world, using it for His purposes to draw all people to Himself.

Israel's experience shows us how God operates. We should pay attention to these things and let them pierce our hearts. The things written beforehand were given as examples for our instruction (1 Corinthians 10:11).

"Return to Me!" God said to Israel. He says it to us today too. Will His words affect our lives, our homes, our churches, our communities? Or do we need to experience what Israel experienced?

SEEK ME
THAT YOU MAY LIVE

The people of Israel had not obeyed God's messages. His warning of judgment came through supernatural events in nature, and now it will come through another nation. He gave Israel chance after chance—He did not give up loving Israel, wanting them to live. His heart is not to destroy them, though many will perish. The day of the Lord will rescue only a few.

DAY ONE

Before beginning your study today, read all of Amos 5 to get the context. Then, read Amos 5:16-27 carefully, marking the key words and phrases from your bookmark. Don't forget to mark *the day of the Lord* as you have done since we started studying Obadiah, Joel, and Amos.

According to verses 16 and 17, how great will Israel's calamity be when the Lord passes through their midst in judgment?

In your notebook, list what you learn from marking *hate* in Amos 5:1-27. Who hates what and why?

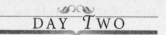

DAY TWO

Once again God speaks of the day of the Lord. What does the text imply about the day of the Lord? What does God want His people to understand? Will this day be a positive or negative experience for them?

Add what you learn to the DAY OF THE LORD chart on pages 26-27.

According to verses 22-24, what does God want the Israelites to stop, and what does He want to see?

What insight do you get from the reference to the wilderness wandering in verses 25-27? Was everyone worshipping God only? What or whom were they worshipping according to verse 27?

Compare Amos 5:27 with Deuteronomy 4:19; Job 9:9; 38:31-33; and Amos 5:8. What insights do you have? Should you consult horoscopes?

Now compare Amos 5:26 with Stephen's message to the leaders of Israel in Acts 7:39-43, which he spoke just before they stoned him to death.

Where are God's people going to go into exile? Read verse 27 carefully and then look up the area on the map THUS SAYS THE LORD TO…on page 63. Note the direction of their captivity with respect to the location of the northern kingdom.

DAY THREE

Now let's move on to Amos 6, the concluding chapter of this segment. Read Amos 6:1-7. Using the locations mentioned in verse 1, identify whom is being addressed. Then read these verses again and mark the key words on your bookmark plus any references to these people. Also mark geographical references.

How would you characterize these people? What do they have, and how do they act? What will happen to them because of their attitude?

DAY FOUR

Today read Amos 6:8-14 and mark key words from your bookmark as well as geographical references.

Now go back and read Amos 5:14-27. What comparison can you make to Amos 6:8-14?

"Lodebar" means "a thing of nothing," and "Karnaim" means "a pair of horns." Are these the names of separate cities, or is God applying the meanings generally to all the cities of Israel? From the context, how do these meanings help you understand what God is saying to Israel?

DAY FIVE

The Hebrew word translated "citadels"[11] in Amos 6:8 is *armon,* which means fortified dwelling, like a palace or castle. Amos uses it 12 times, more than any other writer in the Bible.

Mark *citadel* in Amos 6:8 and then go back and read Amos 1–3, marking *citadels.* How important are the citadels of all these nations to God?

Read Lamentations 2:5,7 and Jeremiah 17:27 and compare to Amos 6:8. Jeremiah wrote 130 years after Amos.

From the writings of Jeremiah, do Judah and Jerusalem appear to have heeded Amos's prophecy?

DAY SIX

Read Amos 5–6 again, looking for Israel's sins and their attitude toward sins. Then read Ezekiel 9 and consider what happens to those who grieve over sin and those who don't.

What are the lessons for us? Can you see parallels in our nation?

Finally, think through Amos 5–6 and decide what the theme of each chapter is. Then record them on AMOS AT A GLANCE on page 111.

Now that you've recorded themes for chapters 3 through 6, you've completed your study of the second segment of Amos. Mark the end of this segment and then record on AMOS AT A GLANCE what this segment is about.

DAY SEVEN

Store in your heart: Amos 5:4
Read and discuss: Amos 5:1-3,10-13; 6:4-8

QUESTIONS FOR DISCUSSION OR INDIVIDUAL STUDY

∾ How does God feel about sin?

∾ What does God do about sin?

- ∞ Does God deal fairly with everyone's sin?

- ∞ What do you need to know and do to avoid God's judgment on sin?

- ∞ Does God want to judge people who sin?

- ∞ From Amos, what specific sins will God judge? Have you committed any of these?

- ∞ How does sin in your nation, city, and community affect you?

- ∞ Do you identify with God's attitude toward sin? Do you share His hatred? His grief?

- ∞ What do you have to do to be like God with respect to sin? How do you know what sin is? What are some practical things in your life you can do?

THOUGHT FOR THE WEEK

As you saw, Amos 5 is a dirge (a lament or a poem of grief). In Amos 6:6, the charge against Judah was clear—they had not "grieved over the ruin of Joseph."

Have you ever stopped to think, Beloved, about the effect our sin has on God? Two verses are instructive: Isaiah 63:10 and Ephesians 4:30. Both speak of grieving the Holy Spirit.

Isaiah 63:10 says that in spite of God's love for Israel and all that He had done for them, they rebelled against Him— they transgressed His Law. Their sin grieved His Holy Spirit.

Ephesians 4:30 instructs the church to not grieve the Holy Spirit by sinning. What's the common thread? Whether we speak of Israel of old or the church today, when God's people sin, He is grieved. God has not changed—He is the same yesterday, today, and forever. Sin has always grieved God; it still does, and it always will.

No wonder Jesus was grieved as He prayed in the Garden of Gethsemane. He knew He was about to die a horrible death by crucifixion for the sins of the whole world. On the cross, He bore all the sins of all men past, present, and future. Because God cannot look upon sin, for that moment the Son grieved the Father. Jesus, sinless at birth and throughout His human life, became sin. And although His Father never stopped loving Him, our sin, which God laid on Him, grieved His Father.

The God who gave His Son to bear our sin, to die on the cross for that sin, to redeem us from slavery to sin by His shed blood, is grieved by our sin today. Jesus paid the price so that we do not pay the penalty of eternal separation from God, and that price was costly. So when we sin, we grieve the Father.

So then, if we love the Father, how should we respond to sin? If our hearts reflect the heart of God the Father, won't we grieve over our sin and the sins of members of our families, communities, and nations? God does!

Ezekiel 9 shows us what God desires. Remember that God told a man with a writing case to mark those who groaned over sin so they would be protected from the coming destruction. What a great contrast this is to the ones in Revelation who are marked with the mark of the beast. *They* go to destruction.

If you had been in Jerusalem in Ezekiel's days, would you have been marked? Intellectually knowing that sin is wrong or "hating the sin but loving the sinner" are not enough. We must grieve over sin as God does so that we have the same urgency about ourselves that Ezekiel, Amos, Obadiah, and Joel had for God's people in their days. If our hearts are one with God, we are motivated to do all we can to declare the truth about sin.

The wages of sin is death. Yet God does not wish that any should perish. Do we want the same thing God wants? What do our actions reveal about us? How serious are we for the business of God to declare sin as sin? Will we stand up for righteousness in an evil and perishing world and say, "Thus says the Lord?" Amos did.

A Plumb Line

A plumb line is a piece of lead (*plumbum* is the Latin word for lead) suspended from a string, cord, or chain that hangs perfectly straight so you can measure against true vertical. Builders use them. Surveyors use them. Wallpaper hangers use them. God uses one. His Word is the plumb line of truth we're all measured against.

DAY ONE

Having thoroughly confronted Israel with its sins and His righteous judgments on the surrounding nations, God now brings consequences. Sin, Beloved, is never without consequence. Read Amos 7 today, marking the key words on your bookmark. Include the phrase *thus the Lord God showed me* and *behold*. These words (and similar ones that indicate the Lord is showing Amos something) mark Amos 7 as the start of a new segment. Similar phrases appear again in Amos 8–9.

Note Amos's role in this chapter and how he intercedes. Remember who this man is and where he's from. Mark every reference to him in a distinctive way.

Note the pattern in these verses. You can mark, color, underline, or do whatever helps you see the pattern. You can also write something in the margin of your Bible to show the repetition.

DAY TWO

Now, let's look more carefully at the first vision, Amos 7:1-3. What did God use to bring righteous judgment to Israel? Read Amos 3:6; 4:9; and Joel 1:1-12. If you studied Joel, this is review. If not, this will help you understand what's going on. God uses repetition to help people remember.

Now read the article on locusts on pages 43–45. You might also read the anecdote in the Thought for the Week on page 36.

DAY THREE

In the vision of Amos 7:4-6, what does God use to bring righteous judgment against Israel?

Fire is a common judgment from God: Read Genesis 19:24-25; Deuteronomy 32:21-22; Psalm 11:4-6; 80:14-19; Joel 1:19-20; and Revelation 8:6-7 for examples. Here in Amos it has been common too.

When you marked *citadels,* did you notice how they would be destroyed? If not, read Amos 1:3–2:5 and mark *fire.*

Now, what pattern is emerging from these first two visions? Write it in your notebook. God sent…then Amos says…then the Lord…

What does this tell you about intercession? Read Numbers 21:7; 1 Samuel 2:25; Isaiah 53:12; Romans 8:26-27,34; and Hebrews 7:25. Amos interceded for Israel. Who has interceded for you, and who will intercede for you today and tomorrow?

DAY FOUR

In Amos 7:7-9, what did God bring against Israel?

Whom does God say He will rise up against? Read Amos 1:1 again. Understanding the historical context is important when the Bible uses a name like this. If you don't remember what you learned in week one, then look again at the historical chart THE RULERS AND PROPHETS OF AMOS'S TIME on page 63.

In Amos 7:11, what two things did Amos say would happen?

In Amos 7:10-13, how does Amaziah's response to Amos support what God said to Israel through Amos in Amos 2:12?

When Amaziah tells Amos to go to Judah, eat bread, and do his prophesying, he may be implying that Amos was simply a "prophet for hire." After all, were all who claimed to be prophets sent from God? This is important for us to know because of the many self-proclaiming prophets and prophetesses today. Look up the following verses and see what you learn. Watch for the consequences of prophesying falsely and listening to false prophecies: Ezekiel 13:17-20; Jeremiah 14:13-16; 23:16-18,21-22,25-32; Micah 3:5,11.

Let's stop for the day and let all these things sink in, Beloved. Tomorrow we'll pick up where we left off.

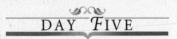

DAY FIVE

In Amos 7:14-17, how does Amos respond to Amaziah? Why wasn't Amos intimidated? List your insights in your notebook. You know, writing out your answers is a good idea because it helps seal truth in your memory. Writing is part of how we learn. We pray that you keep notebooks with your insights in them.

Read Matthew 10:24-28 and 2 Timothy 4:1-5. Note what we're supposed to give people. What does Amos say about this? How can you apply this to your life?

Remember what you saw in Jeremiah 23 yesterday? What does straw have in common with grain? Look up the following scriptures and see what they tell you about the Word of God: John 6:63; 7:17 (you looked up this earlier, but review is good!); 2 Timothy 3:16-17; Hebrews 1:1-2; 4:12. Give people the bread of life—the Word; it will do its job.

DAY SIX

List in your notebook the four things from Amos 7:17 that would happen to Amaziah because he told Amos not to prophesy the Word of God.

Read Acts 4:1-20. What should you do if someone from a rival religion tells you to stop speaking about the Word of God?

When you stand firmly against opposition and threats, who is your ultimate defender? Who renders justice?

Aren't we strengthened in our inner man when we hear the stories of others who have stood firm in the face of threats? Consider reading about the lives of saints and martyrs. You'll draw strength from them. People are dying for their faith today too. Press on, Beloved, press on!

Finally for today, determine the theme of Amos 7 and add it to AMOS AT A GLANCE.

DAY SEVEN

 Store in your heart: Amos 7:15

Read and discuss: Amos 7:1-17; Acts 4:19-20

QUESTIONS FOR DISCUSSION OR INDIVIDUAL STUDY

- Discuss the three visions the Lord showed Amos.

- What were the common elements in the first two visions?

- What do you learn about God from these first two visions? What do you learn about intercession?

- Discuss the plumb line from the third vision. Does God mean a plumb line of lead and string or another kind? What is the plumb line God uses?

- What do you think of Amos's courage? Where does he get this confidence?

ை Discuss Acts 4:19-20 and its parallel in Amos 7:12-17. What should you do? What *will* you do?

ை If you know of any who have stood against warnings not to share the gospel (whether they were just threatened or actually martyred), share those stories with the group.

THOUGHT FOR THE WEEK

If you study Kings and Chronicles, you'll see that Amos was a true prophet. Oh, Beloved, never underestimate the power of God's Word! As Isaiah wrote, God's Word will not return to Him void—it will accomplish His purposes. So give people the Word whether they believe it or not; it will accomplish its purpose in their lives.

As you saw in your study, God uses His Word as the plumb line (standard, benchmark) against which He will measure and judge every person. God says in His Word that we should love our enemies, and we will be measured against that truth. God says in His Word we are to make disciples, so we will be measured against that truth. God says in His Word that He offers only one way to be saved—through faith in the gospel of Jesus Christ. All mankind will be measured against that truth.

A generation is living today that does not believe in absolute truth. It has been indoctrinated by education and society in general to believe that we each have and even *make* our own reality—our own truth and morals.

The sad and most worrisome aspect of this is that many of those who believe this are *young people who claim to be Christians.* In their worldview, holding contradictory beliefs is valid. They do not believe in absolutes. Because their personal belief system includes distorted views of God, their entire worlds are out of plumb. You see, "God" and "world" go *or go out* together!

What can we do? Should we do anything? Should we shrug our shoulders and say, "Oh well, I can't fix it"? Or do we believe that each of us can be an Amos—not a prophet or a son of a prophet, but a shepherd and grower of figs. "The Lord GOD has spoken, who can but prophesy?" (Amos 3:8).

But how do we acquire the truth to be able to declare it? Bible study. The Bible is God's revelation to mankind, recorded by holy men of God moved by the Holy Spirit. It is the plumb line, the truth, true vertical; it is what we must declare in every situation—the "whole counsel" of it (Acts 20:27 NKJV).

You are now studying one booklet from the New Inductive Study Series, which will eventually cover all 66 books of the Bible. God gave us 66 books in our Bible, and every one is important. Together they are the entire revelation of God to man. This series will enable you to see for yourself what the Bible says and means, book by book.

If you wish to go into more depth book by book, then Precept Ministries International recommends its Precept Upon Precept series.

If you want to establish your children in the Bible, you can use the Discover 4 Yourself Bible study series. Children (age eight or above, usually) dig in for themselves and learn *how* to study the Bible *while* they study the Bible. Prepare your children with the plumb line of God, Beloved. Do it yourself at home with them; don't entrust this responsibility to others.

For those who have little time, we have our 40-Minute Bible Studies, which require no work outside of the 40-minute class that meets once a week for six weeks. This series addresses topics that are vital to our lives.

Precept also hosts training seminars, conferences, conventions, study trips to biblical lands, and television and radio programs that give people everywhere, of any age and any language, opportunities to discover truth for themselves from the Word of God, the plumb line, anytime and anywhere.

This is our consuming passion because for more than 35 years of ministry we have seen the Word of God produce incredible enduring fruit in the lives of multitudes. How thrilled we are to have the privilege of studying God's Word with you, Beloved. We pray that our relationship in the Word will continue through all 66 books of the Bible.

A Famine
for the Word

A famine was coming, not a famine of bread or water but of hearing the words of the Lord. O Lord, spare us—spare us from such a famine.

DAY ONE

The Lord God gives Amos another vision in Amos 8:1-3. Read this section and mark key words and phrases as you have done before. Then compare the last sentence of Amos 8:2 with Amos 7:3,6,8. What time phrase is in Amos 8:3 that is not in Amos 7:8?

Read Amos 8:4-6, and then number in the text or list in your notebook the things Israel is doing. How do their actions show their heart? What do you learn about the attitude of their hearts toward the Law of God? Does anything like this go on today?

Do our deeds have anything to do with our faith? Look up the following verses from the Gospel of Matthew and Titus and see what God's Word says: Matthew 7:15-23; Titus 1:16; 2:11-14; 3:5,8,14.

Now, what does your life say about the genuineness of your faith?

DAY TWO

Read Amos 1:1 and 8:7-10. What does Amos 8:7-8 describe? Apparently, what other event follows?

Read Amos 8:7-10 again and mark references to the Lord—what He will do and when. Then add what you find in these verses to your DAY OF THE LORD chart on pages 26–27. Also add what you find in Amos 8:3.

Finally, read and mark Amos 8:11-14. What tragedy does Amos 8:11-13 describe? Why does it happen?

Compare Amos 8:11-13 with Amos 2:4. When we reject God's Law, does God continue to speak?

What do you learn from Amos 8:14? Compare 1 Kings 12:28-30 with Hosea 8:1-6 and 2 Kings 10:21. How did Israel replace God? What did they worship? How did that affect their hearts?

DAY THREE

Does your spirit feel heavy in the light of all this judgment—the tragedy of apostasy? Be cheered, Beloved; a light is at the end of the tunnel.

Read Amos 9:1-10 today, marking key words and phrases as before. Be sure you mark references to the Lord in these verses. Again, Amos has a vision, but this one is different. What makes it different?

Read Amos 9:1-4 again, and mark or list (or both) what the Lord says He will do "though"[12] the fugitives try to hide from Him.

Also note the places where God will find them. Read Psalm 139:7-16 and Hebrews 4:13. Can people hide anything from God? Can man escape what God has ordained?

DAY FOUR

When you study the Word of God, learn all you can about God the Father, the Son, and the Holy Spirit. The people who know their God are able to stand firm and take the right kind of action. Therefore read through Amos 9:1-10 again and look for references to God. Focus on Him and what you learn about Him from the text.

What stands out to you about God in these verses? Write your findings in your notebook.

When you read verse 7, did you notice how the Lord has changed people groups? Read Genesis 10:14; Jeremiah 47:4; and Zephaniah 2:5 to learn more about Caphtor, which many people believe to be Crete.

Now read Amos 1:5 and Isaiah 15:1 to see where Kir is. Moab is in the modern country of Jordan.

Look at what the apostle Paul says on his first visit to Athens. Read Acts 17:24-27. Record your insights in your notebook.

Now, what does such information tell you about God? And what did you just see about Him* again in Amos 9:5-6?

---

* LORD or GOD in small capital letters signifies His most holy and sacred name: YHWH, or Yahweh. Yehowah (We would say Jehovah) comes from the vowel points under Adonai imposed on the tetragrammaton, YHWH, which itself comes from *hayah,* meaning to be, to exist. God is the self-existent One. This name first appears in Genesis 2:4. The Jews called it "the name" or "the great and terrible name, the unutterable name."

Now, look at Amos 9:8-10 more closely. If you didn't mark *sin* when you observed the chapter yesterday, stop and do it now before you go any further.

Does this chapter promise any relief for Israel or offer any hope?

Where is Israel going? What does this tell you about the north as a kingdom?

What does this tell you about Israel (Jacob) as a nation?

What will happen to the sinners? Were any righteous people among them? Think this through from what you studied in Amos.

DAY FIVE

Today read Amos 9:11-15 and mark as usual.

What is the promise, the sure hope, in Amos 9:11-15? List the details in your notebook.

If you haven't studied 1 Kings, you may not be familiar with God's promise to raise up "the fallen booth[13] of David," so let's take a few minutes to look at it. If you have studied it, refresh your memory. Remember, review is an integral part of memory. As you look at these passages, don't miss marking references to time.

Read 2 Samuel 7:8-13. What is God's covenant promise to David?

Now look at 2 Chronicles 13:4-5 and what Abijah, the king of Judah, told Jeroboam I.

Read Jeremiah 33:14-26. This is awesome because it takes us up to our Lord Jesus Christ! Note the repeated use of *covenant*—mark it in your Bible.

Look at Acts 2:29-36 in respect to Jesus being the One who would establish David's throne forever. Record your insights. (Oh, isn't all this glorious? Aren't you amazed at how the Word of God fits together?)

In using the Scripture to prove that God is also going to save Gentiles, James quotes Amos 9 in Acts 15. Acts 15:14-18 proves that the Gentiles can seek and find the Lord, but note that it also supports the fact that God is not finished with Israel, the "tabernacle of David."

God's choice of words show how low His covenant people have fallen. The Hebrew word for "booth" in Amos 9:11 is *succah*—a temporary structure an Israelite family lived in at the Feast of Booths or Tabernacles. This compares with *beth*—a permanent dwelling place.

What is the awesome promise of Amos 9:12? What does this tell you about Israel's status or condition when the Messiah comes to take the throne of David?

DAY SIX

What is God letting the people know in Amos 9:13? Also, do you remember the expression, "the mountains will drip sweet wine"? Sound familiar? Look at Joel 3:18.

What is God's promise to His people Israel in verses 14-15? Summarize it. Also note *why* the land is Israel's. (*Land* refers to Israel, so mark it in a distinctive way. Continue to do so as you read your Bible. It's an important land— according to God's Word in Leviticus, it's *His* land!)

Now, did you notice "they will not again be rooted out from their land which I have given them"? When you continue to study the history of Israel, you will see that they returned to the land (the book of Ezra gives us the account) and remained there until the destruction of Jerusalem in AD 70, when they were dispersed once again among the nations. But in 1948 Israel was reconstituted as a nation.

Now, in accordance with the accuracy of the Word of God (How God watches over His Word to fulfill it!), when is Amos 9:13-15 fulfilled?

Now determine the themes of Amos 8–9 and record them on AMOS AT A GLANCE. Then look at this last segment (Amos 7–9) and record its theme. Lastly, review your chart, determine an overall theme for Amos, and record that on AMOS AT A GLANCE.

Record anything else you'd like on the chart, including such items as the author, historical information, the author's purpose in writing, and key words.

DAY SEVEN

 Store in your heart: Amos 9:11

Read and discuss: Amos 8:7-14; 9:7-15; Acts 15:17

QUESTIONS FOR DISCUSSION OR INDIVIDUAL STUDY

∾ What kind of day will "that day" be?

∾ What does a "famine for hearing the words of the Lord" mean?

∾ How does this kind of famine relate to idolatry?

∾ What parallels can you make today? What should we who have the Word of God be careful to do?

- ∽ Discuss what will happen to the fallen booth of David in the day of the Lord.

- ∽ What will life be like in "their land" in that day? Where is "their land"?

- ∽ Who will be in this group that is "raised up"? What is their relationship to those in Amos 8:11-14?

- ∽ Have these events already taken place, or will they be fulfilled in the future?

- ∽ What does this have to do with Gentiles?

- ∽ What impact do these events have on the church? Should we do anything?

THOUGHT FOR THE WEEK

God said He would bring a famine in the land, not for food and water but for the Word of God. God used ordinary famines many times to further His plans for His people. For example, the famine in Egypt in the days of Joseph was part of God's plan to build a great nation out of the descendants of Abraham. The famine in Bethlehem in the days of Ruth was part of God's plan to bring a Gentile woman into the lineage of David—the "family tree" of Jesus.

Sometimes famines drew people back to dependence on God, giving them a second chance at obedience to Him. Joel and Amos both record famines with this purpose—one caused by a plague of locusts, the other by drought. Israel had forsaken God.

When people forsake God, they replace Him with something else—an idol they will resort to. Those who do not find satisfaction in God are always hungering and thirsting for something to fill the void—the vacuum only He can fill. The tragedy is not only that they will never find true satisfaction apart from Him but also that they will reap the awful judgment of rejecting Him.

Amos declared God's judgment on His people Israel, both the northern and southern kingdoms, because they had forsaken Him and His word. They had voluntarily turned away from God and His word to chase after other gods and worship idols. Now God said that when they wanted His word they would not find it. He would create in them a desire for something they would not be able to get.

As harsh as this seems, it's this final famine that draws the remnant to faith. The fallen booth of David will be restored. Israel will again dwell on their land and in their cities. But the price they will pay beforehand is staggering.

The day of the Lord is not a day of rejoicing for Israel but a day of darkness and judgment. Israel's remnant will be victorious in the end, but it will be a terrible day of reckoning for the rest. Is it possible to avoid this time? Can anyone escape?

Jesus said, "Whoever drinks of the water I will give him shall never thirst; but the water that I will give him will become in him a well of water springing up to eternal life" (John 4:14). He also said, "I am the bread of life; he who comes to Me will not hunger, and he who believes in Me will never thirst" (John 6:35).

There is one way out—one way only for everyone, Jew or Gentile, and that is faith alone in Christ Jesus alone. God has by grace provided a way of escape from the awful judgment of the day of the Lord. This is the grace and love of our God.

How we look forward to the day when God's covenant people will be in their land, living in His presence! And just think: Where Jesus is, we will be also; we'll be with Him. O glorious day!

Amos at a Glance

Theme of Amos:

Segment Divisions

		Chapter Themes
		1
		2
		3
		4
		5
		6
		7
		8
		9

Author:

Date:

Purpose:

Key Words:

Amos

Israel

land

nations (other than Israel)

Edom

covenant

any reference to the name of the Lord

any reference to famine

JONAH

INTRODUCTION TO JONAH

The book of Jonah contains one of the best-known stories in the Old Testament. Teachers draw many object lessons from it in children's ministry, Sunday school, and vacation Bible school. Its popularity is certainly due to the interesting scenario in the belly of a sea creature (fish or whale), but we also appreciate the simple truth about God's grace that brings a person back who's running away, giving him a second chance.

But this story contains many truths. It is quite deep (pun intended) in theological truth, but we need to understand the historical context of Jonah the prophet to appreciate most of it. Some people debate the date that the book was written, but internal evidence in the Bible tells us that Jonah lived during the reign of Jeroboam II of Israel, between 784 and 772 BC.

Assyria was situated north of Aram, east of the Syrian desert, northwest of Babylon, and west of Persia. Its kings resided in the principal cities: Nineveh, Assur, and Calah. At its apex, it included most of the modern countries of Turkey, Syria, Iraq, Lebanon, Israel, and Egypt. The Bible makes no mention of Assyria in the years from David to Jeroboam II, but archaeology has uncovered Assyrian records that mention kings of Israel paying tribute.

Assyria had been an enemy of Israel and would continue to be. God knew that Assyria would carry the last of Israel into captivity in 722 BC. How could God offer salvation to this enemy of His chosen people? Why wouldn't He destroy them?

You'll have to study Jonah to get the answers. Discover them for yourself!

WHAT WOULD JONAH DO?

~~~~~~~~

When God tells us to do something we don't want to do or go somewhere we don't want to go, we might be tempted to run in the other direction. Jonah was human, weak, and imperfect in his obedience to God. But he knew God, and God knew him and chose him to be His special agent in His plan for people. What would Jonah do?

DAY ONE

Read Jonah 1:1-9 and mark the following key words: *Jonah, Lord,* and references to *prayer,* such as *cried* or *call, perish,*[1] *calamity,*[2] and *great.*[3] Make a bookmark on a piece of paper or index card, recording these words and how you will mark them. This will help you be consistent. You might mark *Lord* with a purple triangle, colored inside in yellow. Circle references to prayer in purple and shade the inside in pink. You can use many color and shape combinations to be distinctive. Double underlining in green works well for geographical references.

Don't miss time references in these verses. Some of them show event sequences. If you don't recall how to mark these, refer to "How to Get Started" on page 5.

DAY TWO

Read Jonah 1:1-9 again. Now read 2 Kings 14:23-25; Joshua 19:10,13; and Isaiah 9:1. What do you learn about who Jonah was and where he was from (his city, tribe, and region)? Locate these places on the map below.

Now think through the following questions and record your answers in your notebook. (Remember, writing is part of learning!) What terrible task had God asked Jonah to do? Read Psalm 135:5-6. What did the Lord do? Why?

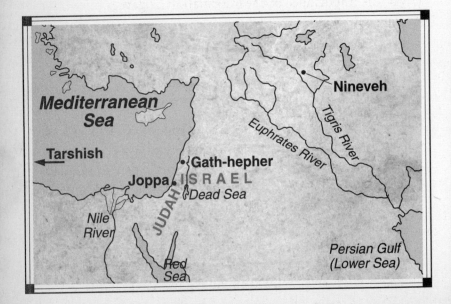

Now, let's carefully go through events and think through implications of what we observed. What was the sailors' first reaction? What does this show you about their relationship to their god?

What was their second reaction? What does this show you about their god's response and their confidence in him?

What did the captain try? What do you learn about his idea of gods?

When they couldn't save themselves, what did the crew do? (We'll take a closer look at this subject tomorrow.)

Read Jonah 1:7-9 again closely. Why did the crew cast lots? What did they ask Jonah first? What did they expect from him?

Now, look at the rest of the questions the sailors asked Jonah. What did they consider important?

What answer did Jonah give? Considering the silence the captain and crew had already received from *their* gods, what was the importance of the information he gave?

DAY THREE

Casting lots in Old Testament times was a means of selecting. Lots could be marked pieces of wood, stone, or bone that would be shaken in a container. The first piece to fall out indicated who was chosen. The Israelites also used the Urim and Thumim, which were kept in a pouch in the breastpiece of the high priest. Read the description in Exodus 28:15-30.

Read the following passages about casting lots and then record your insights in your notebook: Leviticus 16:8-10;

Joshua 18:1-6; 1 Chronicles 26:13-16; Nehemiah 11:1; Esther 9:24; Joel 3:3; Obadiah 11; and John 19:24.

Now read Proverbs 16:33; 18:17-18. What do these tell you about lots?

What do the sailors' questions to Jonah imply that they knew about lots? Even though they had their own gods and did not know the true God, the seed of truth about lots extended to their belief system. But what truth about lots did they *not* know?

DAY FOUR

Today read Jonah 1:10-17, marking key words from your bookmark and references to time as you have done before. As you read and mark, ask the 5 W's and an H. Always ask questions of the text as you read. It has the answers; make it come alive!

Read Matthew 8:23-27. What parallels can you draw?

DAY FIVE

Now let's dig in. As before, write your answers and insights in your notebook. In Jonah 1, what is the relationship between verses 9 and 10? What did Jonah say in verse 9 that told the sailors what he was doing?

What were the sailors afraid of? Read Jonah 1:5,10, and 16, and in each case answer the following: Why were the sailors afraid? What were they afraid of? How did they respond? As you read, you may want to mark words for fear: *afraid, extremely frightened,* and *feared.*

The corresponding Hebrew word, *yare* (pronounced yaw ray), had a wide range of meanings including simple fear, awe, and worship. Jonah 1:9 uses this same Hebrew word when Jonah says he "fears"[4] the Lord God of heaven who made the sea and the dry land. Mark *fear* in that verse too.

As you look at the use of *yare* in these contexts, can you discern the sense of the sailors' fear in Jonah 1:5? Is it different in Jonah 1:10? In Jonah 1:16? What sense of fear does Jonah mean?

Now read Deuteronomy 6:12-16; 13:4; 1 Samuel 12:14-15; Job 1:1,8-9; Proverbs 1:7; 9:10. What do you learn about fearing the Lord?

When Jonah told the sailors what they needed to do to calm the seas, what was their response? Did they fear the Lord in the sense of obedience to Him? What were they trying to do?

How did God use the natural world to give them a new perspective of His power? What were they finally driven to do?

And when the sea calmed, what did the sailors do?

DAY SIX

On our last day of studying Jonah 1, let's take a closer look at the importance of calling on God. Read through Jonah 1 again, looking at all the places where you marked references to *calling on* or *crying out to* pagan gods or to the

Lord. Then in your notebook, note what you learn at each place you marked—who cried, to whom, why, and the result.

Now read Deuteronomy 4:7; 1 Kings 18:21-39; Psalm 107:23-31; 145:18-19; and Joel 2:32. Summarize what you learn about calling on God.

When Jonah told the sailors to throw him into the sea, what was their first response? Why did they first row for shore? The text shows the reason they thought they might perish. What was it? *They were not believers*

Read Exodus 23:7; Deuteronomy 21:8-9; Proverbs 6:16-17; Joel 3:19-21; Matthew 27:3-4,24-25; and Luke 23:44-47. Could this truth from God have become widely known and adopted by other peoples? Or might men naturally know what's right? Read Romans 1:18-20 and then record your insights in your notebook.

Finally, record the theme of Jonah 1 on JONAH AT A GLANCE on page 141.

DAY SEVEN

Store in your heart: Jonah 1:9b
Read and discuss: Jonah 1

QUESTIONS FOR DISCUSSION OR INDIVIDUAL STUDY

∾ Briefly review the sequence of events in Jonah 1.

∾ What is significant about the great storm? Who caused it? What is its purpose?

∾ What does this storm tell you about God?

- ❧ Discuss the sailors' response to the storm.

- ❧ How did Jonah respond to the storm? What made the difference?

- ❧ What did you learn about casting lots?

- ❧ What did you learn about calling on the Lord?

- ❧ What application can you make in your life about calling on the Lord?

- ❧ Discuss the various uses of "fear" and their meanings.

- ❧ What can you apply to your own life about the fear of the Lord?

THOUGHT FOR THE WEEK

When the lot fell on Jonah, the sailors asked him why the calamity had struck, what his occupation was, and where he was from—what country and what people.

Here are the direct answers: The storm was his fault, he was a prophet of God from Gath-hepher in Galilee, he was a Hebrew, and he rebelled against a direct order. But Jonah declared that he was a Hebrew who feared the Lord God of heaven, who made the sea and the dry land. At this they were extremely frightened because he had told them that he was fleeing from the presence of the Lord.

The story is not that a God who sees and knows all finally caught him. God knew Jonah was running away and where he was. That's why the storm came. The amazing thing is that Jonah thought he could book passage on a ship going the opposite direction from where God told him to go—and then think God wouldn't know or do anything about it.

Surely the captain and crew wouldn't find out about his reasons for going to Tarshish! Surely he could hide his disobedience from them, couldn't he?

It's not really amazing at all, is it? We do the same thing. God tells us something, and we either don't do it or do the opposite; then we think God doesn't know and that we'll never get caught. No one will know. That's what happens in adultery, pornography, lying, stealing, murder, and every other sin. We think no one will know. But God always knows.

Even if we rationalize that we'll never get caught by people, we ignore the fact that *God* knows. This is amazing. We know God is omniscient, but we still do the things we do as if we won't get caught or suffer consequences.

Fleeing from the presence of God is just plain impossible. You can run, but you can't hide. God will not leave you alone. He will not let you go your own way and find your own way back. He will raise a "storm" in your life to expose your sin. Then he will use those around you to help you get back to Him.

It's as simple as this statement from Numbers 32:23: "Be sure your sin will find you out." God knows, you know, and at some point, someone else will know.

God will give you exactly what you need to bring you back. He will not leave you in a state of disobedience. Because He loves you, because He is a covenant-keeping God, He will use circumstances to turn you around. That is what God has done throughout the history of Israel. He used natural disasters, supernatural miracles, other nations, and prophets of His Word to turn Israel around.

What will He use with you? Will He use the Holy Spirit we are sealed with? Will the abiding presence of God in us prick our conscience and cause us to confess our sin before our gracious heavenly Father? Will we cry out to Him for forgiveness and restoration? Will we cry to Him for strength and courage?

We have the promise in 1 John 1:9 that "if we confess our sins, He is faithful and righteous to forgive us our sins and to cleanse us from all unrighteousness." Will we trust Him and take Him at His Word?

Don't try to flee from His presence the way Jonah did. Run to Him, into His loving arms, because He loves you and will forgive you whatever you confess. You have His Word on it.

WHAT WOULD JONAH PRAY?

When you're caught in a difficult situation where all seems lost, when hope seems beyond reach, what do you do? Do you pray? Too often, prayer is the last resort. We say, "All we can do now is pray." Do we think we must first exhaust all human effort and only then turn to God? That's not the way God sees it. We should pray first, asking what to do. Then, as we do it, we should pray for strength and wisdom. Afterward, we should pray in thanksgiving. What would Jonah do? What would he pray?

DAY ONE

Read Jonah 1:17 again to establish the context of Jonah 2. This verse contains a key word we didn't tell you to mark previously—*appointed.*[5] Mark it in a distinct way and add it to your bookmark. This word doesn't appear again until Jonah 4, where we'll discuss its implications.

In light of what you see in Jonah 1:17, read Jonah 2:1-10 and mark the key words and phrases on your bookmark as you have done before.

Jonah 1 presented Jonah on a ship on the ocean, fleeing from God. What is the setting of Jonah 2?

What is the sequence of events in the chapter? Note them in the margin of your Bible or in your notebook.

DAY TWO

Think about Jonah's state of mind. He had been caught fleeing God. The storm was his fault, so he told the sailors to toss him overboard. What was he thinking? Do you think he thought he deserved to die? What in Jonah 2 helps you answer this question?

Do you think Jonah thought he was going to die after he was thrown overboard? Write in your notebook or Bible what Jonah experienced.

How did Jonah "remember" the Lord? *in prayer*

When Jonah thought he was going to die, what did he say he was going to do? If he was cast out of God's sight, where would he "see" Him? Where is God's holy temple?

Can you see yourself in this situation—drowning and crying out to God? Is God sovereign over all situations?

Read Psalm 8; 42:5-7; 50:14-15,22-23; 95:1-7. Review Psalm 107:23-31 (which you read last week) but this time start in verse 17. What parallels do you see to Jonah's situation in your own? How can you use these or any psalms to pray?

DAY THREE

A variety of theories exist about the "fish" that swallowed Jonah. Some speculate that it was a sperm whale, which would be common in the Mediterranean Sea. Some think it was a whale shark, and others guess a great white shark.

Whales are mammals, and sharks are fish, but all three of these species can swallow a man whole, and large objects have been found in their bellies. The Hebrew word for "fish" allows for either whales or fish as it does in Genesis 1.

But the kind of sea creature that swallowed Jonah and then vomited him is not the point. The bulk of the chapter is about Jonah crying out to God in prayer, as you have seen. Prayer is too large a subject to exhaust in this study, but today let's look a little deeper than we have so far.

Read the following passages and then summarize in your notebook what you learn about prayer: 1 Kings 8:54; Job 42:10; Matthew 6:5-15; Mark 11:25; Romans 8:26; Ephesians 6:18; 1 Thessalonians 5:16-18; 1 Timothy 2:1-4,8; James 5:13-18.

The Bible includes many great prayers to learn from, such as Solomon's prayer at the dedication of the Temple (1 Kings 8:22-54 and its parallel, 2 Chronicles 6:12-42), Daniel's prayer for his people (Daniel 9:3-19), and of course the Psalms. If you have time and want to read these to learn how to pray, do so. You will be blessed.

Record the theme of Jonah 2 on JONAH AT A GLANCE on page 141.

DAY FOUR

Now that Jonah is out of the fish, we'll continue our study. Read Jonah 3 today, marking key words and phrases from your bookmark as you have done before. Mark any geographical references by double underlining them in green and mark time references with a clock as before.

Watch for new characters and add two new key words: *turn*[6] and *relent*.

DAY FIVE

What do you learn about Nineveh from Jonah 3?

Nineveh was so great that it carries the name "the great city" here in Jonah. Genesis 10:11 tells us that Nineveh was one of the cities founded by Nimrod after he left Babylon.

Located on the east bank of the Tigris River across from the modern city of Mosul, Iraq, it is near a main river crossing and leads to the best farmland. The wall around the city was 50 feet high, and although it enclosed a smaller area, if all the "suburbs" around the walled city are included, the city was about 30 miles long along the river by 10 miles deep from the river. The "three days' journey" does not necessarily designate the internal size of Nineveh (its circumference, diameter, or total administrative district); the phrase can tally a day's journey in from the suburbs (see 3:4), a day for business, and a one-day return.

Assyria the nation and Nineveh the great city had many temples to idols, their gods. What was Jonah's message to Nineveh? How does this compare to Jonah 1:1-2?

Read Genesis 6:13; 18:20; 19:12-14,29; Numbers 21:1-3; Deuteronomy 2:19-23; 29:23; Job 12:23; Isaiah 10:24-27; Jeremiah 1:9-10; 50:17-18; Zephaniah 2:13-15; Zechariah 12:9. If you haven't studied Amos, read Amos 1:3–2:3. Make a list showing who has been destroyed, who will be destroyed, and for what reasons.

When Nineveh received Jonah's message, did the people have reason to believe God might destroy the city?

DAY SIX

What was the response of the people of Nineveh to Jonah's message from God?

Fasting, sackcloth, and ashes are mentioned throughout the Old Testament. Today let's look a little more closely at sackcloth and ashes. Next week, we'll pick up where we left off and look at fasting.

Back in the first week of our study of Joel (the second week of this 13-week booklet), we looked briefly at sackcloth, but today we'll look at sackcloth and ashes. To review, read Genesis 37:34; Daniel 9:1-3; Matthew 11:21; and Revelation 6:12. You can look these up or review your notes from Joel.

Here are some additional scriptures that speak of ashes alone or sackcloth and ashes together: 2 Samuel 13:19; Esther 4:1-3; Isaiah 58:5; Jeremiah 6:26; 25:34; and Ezekiel 27:30-31. Read these and then summarize how people used sackcloth and ashes and for what purposes.

Why should the citizens of Nineveh mourn? Had someone died? Read Joel 2:12-13.

What is the reason for wearing ashes on the forehead on Ash Wednesday?

Let's stop there, Beloved, and pick up in chapter 3 next week. We've covered a lot and have much to discuss tomorrow.

DAY SEVEN

 Store in your heart: Jonah 2:9—"Salvation is from the Lord."

Read and discuss: Jonah 2:2,7-9; 3:1-6

QUESTIONS FOR DISCUSSION OR INDIVIDUAL STUDY

- ∾ Discuss Jonah's prayer from the belly of the great fish. Use the 5 W's and an H.

- ∾ What did Jonah now understand that he didn't in Jonah 1:1-3?

- ∾ Relate some personal experiences in which you, like Jonah, "remembered" the Lord in a difficult time and prayed.

- ∾ What does the Lord want from your prayers?

- ∾ What do you think the Lord desires with respect to prayer? Support your answers from Scripture.

- ∾ From Jonah 3:1-6, discuss Nineveh's response to Jonah's preaching.

- ∾ Have you ever seen anything like what happened in Nineveh? Would you like to see a city or nation respond as Nineveh did? Do our cities and nations need to? *Yes*

- ∾ What would be required for your city to respond as Nineveh did? What do *you* need to do?

- ∾ What is your culture's equivalent to sackcloth and ashes? How does this custom show what's going on inside a person?

THOUGHT FOR THE WEEK

God had gotten Jonah's attention. The great wind and the great storm had nearly cost everyone on the ship their lives. Jonah had been sinking in the depths of the ocean, drowning, and the fish swallowed him and saved him. In the belly of the fish for three days and nights, Jonah finally repented. He changed his mind about going to Nineveh.

Sometimes getting our attention is difficult. An old story illustrates this: A man was pulling on the reins of a stubborn mule, but the mule just wouldn't budge. So the man picked up a two-by-four and whacked the mule right between the eyes. The mule dropped to his knees. "What did you do that for?" asked a bystander who had witnessed the scene. "Sometimes you have to get his attention," the man replied.

What does God do to get *your* attention? What's your equivalent of being hit between the eyes with a two-by-four? For many of us, life is routine. We go about our daily business (life as usual) without remembering that God is involved in every detail. God has told us how we should walk, but sometimes we go the opposite way.

What will finally drive us to our knees? Sometimes we need to come to the point where we realize our dependence on God. Something must get our attention, drop us to our knees, and put us into an attitude of prayer. Disease? Death? Accident? Financial ruin? Loss of job? Flood? Tornado? Hurricane? Fire?

What a shame that such a thing would be necessary to get us to pray as we ought, to recognize that salvation is from the Lord. We know these things, but if things are going along well in our lives, our prayer life can suffer.

As children of God, we know we have free access to the throne of grace. We have immediate, dedicated, 24/7 access to God in prayer. It's online all the time.

So pray without ceasing. In all things by prayer and supplication make your requests known to God. How different our lives, families, and communities will be if we get on our knees more often. Our prayers don't have to be eloquent, long, or wordy. But they do need to be frequent, heartfelt, sincere, and fervent. On the National Day of Prayer, are our churches filled to overflowing? Do our nations pray?

For those who name the name of Jesus, every day is a day of prayer. We don't need to go to a special place or set a special time to pray, but when we have the opportunity to pray in public as a witness or testimony to the world around us, we would do well to take it.

Is prayer the first thing we think of doing in a situation? Or is it our last resort? Do we enjoy prayer? It can be hard work, but does communicating with our heavenly Father bring us joy? Do we enjoy praising Him? He takes pleasure in hearing praise; He likes to hear us vocalize our dependence on Him.

Why don't you end today's study in prayer? Right now, right where you are, go before our Father in thanksgiving and praise and then ask Him to help you in something specific.

He'll enjoy hearing from you.

ABUNDANT IN LOVINGKINDNESS

ɔɯɔɯɔɯɔ

When God sees a person humbly bowing before Him, praying for forgiveness, asking Him to relent from His wrath because He is compassionate, because He is gracious, because He is slow to anger and abundant in lovingkindness, He may relent. He did so for Nineveh.

DAY ONE

Let's pick up today where we left off last week in chapter 3. Read Jonah 3:5-10 to refresh your memory. We studied sackcloth and ashes last week, and today we'll look at fasting.

If you studied Joel, you learned about sackcloth and fasting. You can review what you studied there or read the following scriptures to see what we can learn to put into practice. Note who fasted, why and when they fasted, what if anything accompanied their fast, and what kind of fast it was. Also note what happened as a result of the fast: 1 Samuel 7:3-14; 2 Samuel 12:13-23; 1 Kings 21:20-29; Esther 4:13-16; Isaiah 58:1-12; Daniel 9:1-5; Matthew 6:1,16-18; Luke 5:30-35; Acts 13:1-3; 14:23.

How should we approach God to ask Him for His favor? What kind of approach do we see in these passages? Can you understand why God responded to Nineveh as He did?

DAY TWO

We've looked at how man should approach God with fasting, sackcloth and ashes, and prayer, that He might relent and withdraw His burning anger. Does He usually change His mind? Will He relent every time we ask? Read these cross-references: 2 Samuel 24:13-16; Psalm 106:40-48; Jeremiah 15:6; 18:6-10; Ezekiel 24:14; Joel 2:13-14; Zechariah 8:14-17.

But someone might ask, "What about Numbers 23:19 and 1 Samuel 15:29?" Read these verses, but look at the context. The context of Numbers 23 and 1 Samuel 15 should make the answer clear. Read these chapters and then formulate your answer in the context of all the other verses you've studied today.

So does God always relent? What should you do if you want God to relent?

Now that we've finished our study of this chapter, record the theme of Jonah 3 on JONAH AT A GLANCE.

DAY THREE

Now let's move on to Jonah 4 today. Read Jonah 4 and mark the key words and phrases on your bookmark. Add the new key word *angry* (also *anger*). Don't miss *appointed;* mark it the same way you marked it in Jonah 1:17. Also double underline geographical references and mark time references with a clock as you have done before.

DAY FOUR

As we look at Jonah 4, list in your notebook (or the margin of your Bible) major events in the chapter. What happens?

Now go through these events and follow the progress of Jonah's emotions or moods. What did you learn from marking *anger* and *angry*? Why was Jonah angry the first time? Was his anger justified?

Let's look at *anger* a little more closely. Read the following scriptures and summarize in your notebook what you learn about anger: Galatians 5:19-25; Ephesians 4:26-32; Colossians 3:8; James 1:19-20.

What lessons can you draw from these verses and from the book of Jonah?

DAY FIVE

What did you learn from marking *appointed*? Read Jonah 1:17 and list what God appointed. Can you identify any principles about God's appointments? What do you learn about God and creation? God "appointed" a fish, a plant, and a worm to create or change circumstances to carry out His plan just as He hurled a great wind on the sea. God is in control.

This idea occurs elsewhere in the Old Testament and carries over into the New Testament to the church as well. The Hebrew word translated *appointed* here has the idea of assigning a place or commanding, so the sovereignty of God is clear. Only a sovereign can direct such affairs.

What's implied for us? Read the following and then summarize what you learn about God appointing things: John 15:16; Acts 22:12-16; 1 Corinthians 12:28; Hebrews 9:27.

DAY SIX

The last concept we need to look at is compassion. Read through Jonah 4 again and mark *compassion(ate)*. The Hebrew word for *compassionate*[7] in Jonah 4:2 is rooted in the idea of the love of a superior, and it can also be translated as "mercy." The Hebrew word translated "compassion"[8] in Jonah 4:10-11 is "to look on with pity and have mercy." These two attitudes produce the same result—mercy—but they are rooted in two different motivations. Both are used of God, so read the following and then record in your notebook what you learn about the compassion of God: Deuteronomy 4:31; 2 Chronicles 30:9; Nehemiah 9:17; Psalm 86:15; Joel 2:13.

In the New Testament, the Greek word also reflects the idea of mercy. Read Romans 9:15; 12:1; Colossians 3:12; James 5:11.

What place, then, should mercy or compassion have in our lives if we are to reflect God's nature?

Finally, record the theme of Jonah 4 on JONAH AT A GLANCE and then determine an overall book theme and also record it. If you see segment divisions, record them in the appropriate place as you have before. These can be based on changes in things like location, Jonah's activities, or subject matter. Add other notes to the chart such as the author, date, and historical setting.

Congratulations, dear student, you've finished Jonah! And if you've completed the work on all four of the minor prophets in this booklet, then quadruple congratulations are in order!

DAY SEVEN

 Store in your heart: Jonah 4:2b—"You are a gracious and compassionate God."

Read and discuss: Jonah 3:7–4:11

QUESTIONS FOR DISCUSSION OR INDIVIDUAL STUDY

- ∾ Review and discuss the sequence of events from Jonah 3:7 to Jonah 4:11.

- ∾ What do you learn about God from this episode in Jonah's life?

- ∾ Describe the biblical perspective on anger and compassion.

- What have you learned about your emotions and reactions to God's dealings in your life?

- Discuss how God used Jonah for His purposes even though Jonah wasn't perfect.

- Can you identify in any way with Jonah?

- How does the book of Jonah help you to be a better Christian?

- Discuss the "second chances" in Jonah.

THOUGHT FOR THE WEEK

God is gracious and compassionate, slow to anger, abundant in lovingkindness, and One who relents concerning calamity. He looks upon mankind with love as a superior to an inferior, has pity, and extends mercy. He certainly destroyed Sodom and Gomorrah, and Obadiah, Joel, and Amos all prophesied of God's destruction of sinners. Yet, in Nineveh's case, He relented. Why? Because they repented. They turned to God in fasting, sackcloth, and ashes. They humbled themselves before God.

Oh, Beloved, how we must catch this principle! If we really believe that the destruction of the wicked is sure, that sin must be judged by a holy and righteous Judge, then we must be about the Father's business. We do not love our neighbor, we do not love our enemy, we do not love the world as God loves if we do not have the same compassion God has. He extends mercy because of His lovingkindness. He stays His hand from judging because of His great love.

Someone said that we should be like the moon. The moon doesn't *produce* light, but it *reflects* the light of the sun. The Son is Light, and we are not the Son; we reflect the Son's light to others. If that's true, we must be sure to reflect His lovingkindness, slowness to anger, graciousness, and compassion in this world.

How do we do this? The same way the Father did. He sent prophets to tell of the promised Messiah who would save people from their sins. They declared truth to sinners to turn them back to God. They gave people a chance to humble themselves before God with fasting, sackcloth, and ashes to show their repentance, humility, and entreaty to God.

He sent His spokesmen to declare "Thus says the Lord" to a lost and dying generation so that they could be saved. In Nineveh's case, they turned, and God relented. They received a second chance.

So it is with each of us. When we, like the Thessalonians (1 Thessalonians 1:9), turn from idols to serve a living and true God, we turn from death to life. We receive mercy and grace based on the lovingkindness of God.

Catch the reality of what God has done for you, precious one! See the goodness of God and His love for you. Share that truth with others. Be God's spokesman with His truth in your family, church, and community. Spread the good news that Jesus has died for the sins of the world and that whoever believes in Him will be saved.

When Paul ended both his letters to Timothy, he gave a solemn charge and invoked a special condition. We would like to give that same charge to you, Beloved, as we close this study: We charge you *Coram Deo* (Latin for "in the presence of God," literally, "in the face of God") to serve the Lord.

> I solemnly charge you in the presence of God
> and of Christ Jesus, who is to judge the living
> and the dead, and by His appearing and His
> kingdom: preach the word; be ready in season
> and out of season; reprove, rebuke, exhort,

with great patience and instruction. For the time will come when they will not endure sound doctrine; but wanting to have their ears tickled, they will accumulate for themselves teachers in accordance to their own desires, and will turn away their ears from the truth and will turn aside to myths. But you, be sober in all things, endure hardship, do the work of an evangelist, fulfill your ministry (2 Timothy 4:1-5).

Fulfill your ministry, Beloved; preach the Word in season and out; be God's agent for second chances.

Theme of Jonah:

Segment Divisions

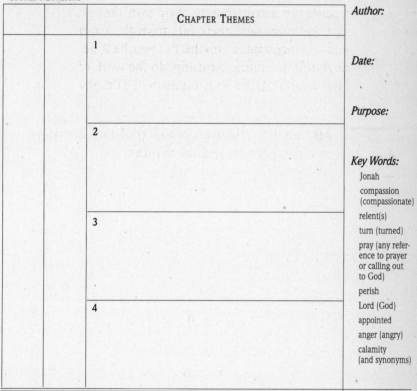

		Chapter Themes
		1
		2
		3
		4

Author:

Date:

Purpose:

Key Words:
Jonah

compassion
(compassionate)

relent(s)

turn (turned)

pray (any refer-
ence to prayer
or calling out
to God)

perish

Lord (God)

appointed

anger (angry)

calamity
(and synonyms)

Notes

Obadiah

1. KJV: the heathen
2. NIV: my holy hill

Joel

1. ESV: hopper, cutter, destroyer; KJV: palmerworm, cankerworm, caterpillar
2. ESV: ground; NIV: ground
3. NIV: hill
4. ESV: northerner
5. KJV: heathen
6. KJV: ghost
7. NIV: distress
8. NKJV: everlasting; KJV: everlasting

Amos

1. NIV: this is what the Lord says; KJV: thus saith the Lord
2. KJV: hath
3. NKJV: says; KJV: saith
4. ESV: this is what the Lord God showed me; NIV: this is what the Sovereign Lord showed me; KJV: That hath the Lord God shewed unto me
5. NIV: sins
6. NIV: sins
7. NIV: false gods
8. NIV: sin
9. NIV: sin
10. KJV: kine

11. ESV: strongholds; NIV: fortresses; NKJV: palaces; KJV: palaces
12. ESV: if
13. NIV: tent; NKJV: tabernacle; KJV: tabernacle

Jonah

1. NIV: die
2. ESV: evil, disaster; NIV: trouble, destruction; NKJV: trouble, disaster; KJV: evil
3. ESV: mighty, exceedingly; NIV: violent, important; NKJV: mighty, exceedingly; KJV: mighty, exceedingly
4. NIV: worship
5. NIV: provided; NKJV: prepared; KJV: prepared
6. NIV: give up
7. ESV: merciful; NKJV: merciful; KJV: merciful
8. ESV: pity; NIV: concerned; NKJV: pity; KJV: pity